New York
Architecture

photographs by Richard Berenholtz
introduction by Carol Willis
text by Amanda Johnson

New York
Architecture

a history

UNIVERSE

First published in the United States of America in 2003
by **UNIVERSE PUBLISHING**
A Division of Rizzoli International Publications, Inc.
300 Park Avenue South
New York, NY 10010

2008 2009 2010 2011 / 10 9 8 7 6 5 4 3

DESIGNED BY Sara E. Stemen

ISBN: 978-0-7893-0-777-4

LIBRARY OF CONGRESS CONTROL NUMBER: 2002112182
www.rizzoliusa.com

IMAGES ON PRECEDING SPREADS:
ii–iii: View across the boat pond to some of the city's most coveted and recognizable high-rise apartment buildings along Central Park West, including the Majestic, the Dakota, and the San Remo Apartments. **i–v:** Skyscrapers close in on the sky in midtown, with the distinctive wedge-top of Citicorp Center at top, center, and the elliptical-plan 895 Third Avenue—known popularly as the Lipstick Building. **vi–vii:** The Empire State Building framed by a Manhattan Bridge support in DUMBO (Down-Under-the-Manhattan-Bridge-Overpass), Brooklyn

In loving memory of my parents, Marjorie and Harry Berenholtz

Contents

Introduction

New York, New York—that is the only thing redundant about it. Change is the norm in this city, and so is diversity. A walk up a midtown avenue, Lexington or Park, for example, makes clear that Manhattan is a place where competition, ambition, and self-promotion act out on every block and lot. Even neighbors of the same era and style, like Lever House and the Seagram Building, compete to be different. New York denies the desire for serene harmonies of London terraces or the boulevards of Paris. Manhattanism, as Rem Koolhaas named it in *Delirious New York*, is a "culture of congestion" and relentless diversity.

So, then, how to fashion a coherent story of New York architecture? Some valiant souls have attempted to make comprehensible the whole in an encyclopedic embrace. Robert A. M. Stern and his team of coauthors organize their series of hefty volumes, *New York 1880, New York 1900*, etc., in decadinal chunks, principally by building types, districts, or boroughs. Another tome, *The Encyclopedia of New York City*, simply employs the alphabet and eschews an overview, while the fat *AIA Guide to New York City* tackles the task by narrating neighborhood walks building by building.

A much more modest method is this sampler of twenty-seven buildings (out of ten thousand times more structures) brought together under the title *New York Architecture*. Ordered chronologically, they span more than a century, from the 1887 Puck Building to the LVMH tower, finished in 2000, and are scattered across the island—Manhattan only is the territory, unless one counts the other ends of the Queensboro and George Washington bridges. They are a grab bag of landmarks united by the gorgeous photography of Richard Berenholtz. His images are monumental, heroic, and silent: hardly any people intrude, even in the great public spaces of Grand Central Terminal or the plaza of Lincoln Center. Berenholtz freezes forms, silhouettes, and surfaces, and he isolates elements—a facade sculpture, a building crown, a window pattern—that stand in for the whole. In our vertical and congested city, structures rarely fit the frame, and we often experience buildings only as tops or bottoms or in partial views from the sidewalk, a taxi, an office window. Just as Berenholtz's photographs of parts give a sense of the full structure, this selection of a couple dozen buildings can describe key characteristics of the city's architecture.

What themes can we find here to illuminate the nature of New York? One essential idea lies in density of development. In the three centuries since its first European settlement as New Amsterdam, Manhattan has been mapped, land-filled, and built over almost completely. The place has become either real estate or public realm—privately developed buildings versus streets, parks, and civic structures. The dynamic of property ownership expanded north, but also, in successive waves of rebuilding, upward into the vertical.

The majority of buildings in this collection are skyscrapers, the quintessential symbol of the city. Even more than Chicago, which generally gets more credit from historians, New York was the birthplace of the skyscraper, and it remains the city where the high rise is a locus of everyday life for millions. Most New Yorkers begin their daily commute on an elevator that takes them down to street level. The enabling mechanism of urban density, the elevator was invented—actually, improved and promoted—in the 1850s in New York by Elisha Graves Otis. It was not, however, introduced into tall office buildings until the 1870s, when for the first time structures began to stretch to ten or twelve stories. New York's first crop of truly tall towers, around sixteen to twenty stories, sprang up in lower Manhattan in the early 1890s, driven higher by demand for prime locations and by the technological revolution of skeleton construction, in which a 3-D grid of steel columns and beams replaced the traditional bearing-wall. Pioneered in Chicago in the 1880s, skeleton construction came late to New York where local architects and engineers had developed hybrid systems of masonry and metal that satisfied the city's conservative building code. When permitted officially, the new structural system allowed interiors to be more open and efficient and also meant the facade was carried on the frame and could become much lighter, a "curtain wall."

Still, the structural revolution did not produce a new aesthetic. Though they quickly embraced technological advances, New York architects remained attached to historical styles and to a richness of ornament expressed in quality materials and elaborate sculptural or artistic programs. This aesthetic of surface richness existed in the masonry era—as in the layered brick of the Puck Building—but it reached an extreme in examples such as the Alwyn Court apartments, laden with heraldic ornament of the early French Renaissance, modeled of glazed terra cotta. The gothic tracery, gargoyles, finials, and tourelles of the Woolworth Building, also molded in terra cotta and glazed white with subtle touches of color, referred to Flemish and French Gothic, a decision made in concert by architect Cass Gilbert and client, five-and-dime tycoon Frank W. Woolworth. The world's tallest building in 1913, employing unprecedented structural engineering and mechanical services, the "Cathedral of Commerce" nevertheless expressed its ambition in a gothic spire.

Civic buildings established a taste for opulence. The very embodiment of the riches of New York at the dawn of the American Century was the U. S. Custom House on Bowling Green, at the head of Broadway. In 1899, the U. S. Department of the Treasury held a competition for a new Custom House, an edifice that would accommodate the growing bureaucratic needs and symbolize New York's status as the great American metropolis. At the time, nearly two-thirds of the country's total imports as well as half its exports passed through the Port of New York, generating a major part of the revenues of the federal government. Competition winner Cass Gilbert (a decade before the Woolworth tower) designed a palatial facade of seven stories, a massive base, a central section unified by a colonnade of colossal Corinthian columns, and an attic zone that multiplied the sculptural program with figures personifying the great sea-faring nations. The elevated entrance presented a daunting flight of stairs, flanked by robust allegorical figures of the continents by the master Daniel Chester French, with North America and Europe to either side and Asia and Africa to the east and west. In the traditional language of European architecture, the U. S. Custom House bespoke the affluence and confidence of New York's real riches and world stature.

—— Wealth entered the city and multiplied not only through its harbor, but by rail. In the first decades of the century, the railroad leviathans the New York Central and the Pennsylvania Railroad erected magnificent stations that ranked among the city's most imposing civic landmarks, though they were built by private capital. Lamentably lost to the wreckers' ball in the 1960s, Pennsylvania Station was designed by McKim, Mead, and White to reproduce the gravitas of imperial Rome and the Baths of Caracalla. At Grand Central Terminal, the Beaux Arts architecture of Warren and Wetmore was more exuberant, as evidenced by the colossal trio of Mercury, Minerva, and Hercules on the Park Avenue pediment. Today the station is embedded in the activity of Forty-second Street and so overpowered by the looming mass of the Met Life tower that its monumentality may elude us. But no one can escape being awestruck upon entering the terminal's main concourse, a majestic room 375 by 120 feet, an acre in area, that soars 125 feet to a vault of blue-green sky painted with constellations. One of the city's greatest public rooms, the Grand Central concourse represents New York's ultimate luxury: open space. Space-making at this scale is very unusual in Manhattan—a theme we will take up later.

Monumentality, material richness, and indulgence in lavish ornament became characteristic of New York architecture through the first half of the twentieth century. For skyscrapers, an aesthetic of massive scale was hardly a stretch. Within our group of buildings, the Con Edison Company Building was a sort of super-sized version of the memorial erected as Grant's Tomb. The tower top was based on the Mausoleum of Halicarnassus and featured urns, torches, and other classical motifs of gigantic proportions. In the Hearst Building of 1930, architect Joseph Urban used the classical language in a modern idiom for the building's massive base; now, some seventy years later, a tower is finally to be added by Foster and Associates. Many other skyscrapers not illustrated here belong to this classical family—the 1912 Banker's Trust tower at Wall and Nassau streets, the Standard Oil Building at 26 Broadway, and Equitable Life Assurance at 15 Broad Street, for example. The office towers of the downtown financial district in particular favored a monumental, institutional appearance. In the 1920s, this sensibility was reinforced by the city's zoning law of 1916, which dictated a setback form for tall buildings that gave them the form of a great stepped pyramid.

Limestone was also a leitmotif through the thirties. The favorite for public architecture, the material is beautifully uniform, durable, and can be carved into richly three-dimensional decoration. Expensive, even when used only in thin slabs as curtain wall cladding, limestone suggests a quality project. Developers or institutions often specified it to their architects. Two cases in point were the Empire State Building and Rockefeller Center. In an article in 1931, William Lamb, chief designer of the Empire State, described five points of the program given by the clients, the fourth being "an exterior of limestone." Indeed, the tower shows more stone that steel on its face, as all the surface that was not within the vertical bands of the windows is limestone cladding, installed as standardized panels. The decision to use stone to face the seventy-story RCA Building at Rockefeller Center and the later buildings of the complex was credited to John D. Rockefeller, Jr., whose preference for masonry was also evidenced in two of his philanthropic projects of the period, the construction of the English Gothic Riverside Church and the reconstruction of the medieval Cloisters. The three-block ensemble of Rockefeller Center creates a canyon of limestone that, although called conservative in its day, has aged in critical admiration and is regarded as a paragon of urban design.

The other characteristic materials of New York architecture through the first decades of the century were brick, terra cotta, and glass—the latter for windows, but not yet for walls, as in its postwar development. Brick was the backdrop of the urban fabric. Less expensive than stone, and cheaper to construct, brick was available in a range of colors; in gray or beige it often lent the appearance of stone and was used in combination with masonry or terra-cotta details. Red brick never went out of style, but it enjoyed particular popularity in the 1880s, when the round-arched Romanesque Revival was in vogue, as in the Puck Building and other commercial lofts in Soho and Tribeca. It was also used as the background color for the tower of the Singer Building, tallest in the world in 1908. In the 1920s, brick was the dominant material for curtain-wall cladding in most high rises, sometimes with coloristic effects of shading from dark to light brick as the building rose, or with a surface pattern in the wall or the spandrel, the area directly below the window. The Chrysler Building employed pattern in subtly woven horizontals and verticals on its base section, as well as in bold black bands that tied together rows of windows in the tower and wrapped around corners with a streamlined effect. Glazed brick, in white and black as at the Chrysler Building or the nearby Daily News, gave the towers the taut and planar appearance associated with the modern style.

"Terra-cotta skyline" is an apt description of New York in the early twentieth century and the title of a wonderful history by Susan Tunick of the once ubiquitous material. Architectural terra cotta was popular for ornament or full curtain walls from the late nineteenth century through the 1930s. Made of fired clay, unglazed or glazed, terra cotta had multiple virtues: it was easy to mold into complex forms to create specialized or mass-produced ornament; it could masquerade as masonry at a fraction of the price; and it was fireproof. Several buildings in this book display the protean range of terra cotta. The Bayard Condict Building of 1899, the only New York design by the Chicago master Louis Sullivan, illustrates the extreme of individual expression. The frieze of angels, interlacing foliage, and thin colonettes with sprouting tendrils, all in cream-colored terra cotta, imparted both delicacy and energy and were boldly original. By contrast, the facade of the Flatiron Building constituted a gallery of classical motifs, with every surface embellished, although the stone-gray panels blended into an overall surface texture. Likewise, the Alwyn Court dripped with dragons, putti, cartouches, candelabra, and fleurs de lis. A different direction was developed in 1930 in the McGraw-Hill Building (now called the Group Health Insurance Building), where architect Raymond Hood wrapped his setback skyscraper in blue-green tiles like a terra-cotta skin. Alas, the potential for crayon-colored skyscrapers that might have advanced after Hood broke the barrier did not, though, because the Depression and World War II halted most commercial construction.

The issue of modernism in New York is complex. Many critics and historians have called the city's architecture conservative for its attachment to historical styles. But how does one define modern? The gothic spire of the Woolworth Building ascended to 792 feet, more than four hundred feet higher than Chicago's tallest tower of the time. To reach that altitude required considerable invention—advances in foundation engineering, windbracing, steel erection, elevatoring, mechanical systems, and so on. At Grand Central Terminal, the Beaux Arts architecture was less remarkable than the hidden technology of the electrified trains, suppressed for several miles in an open cut that within a decade was completely built over with the luxury buildings of Park Avenue. Skyscrapers, subways, power stations—New York was unwittingly modern.

From the mid-1920s, many New York architects searched for a vocabulary to define a modern style. Influenced by fashions in Europe, but also intent on identifying American sources, they developed what today is called Art Deco, an aesthetic that turned away from historical reference, but not from richness of surfaces, materials, and elaborate murals and sculpture. The epitome of the style was the Chrysler Building. Stainless steel eagle heads at the upper-level setbacks, silver scallops of the telescoping crown of the tower, the rainbows of triangular windows, a sumptuous lobby of colored marbles, decorative wood inlays on the elevator doors and cabs, uplifting murals of construction workers and the city on the rise—the Chrysler Building displayed an endearing appetite for overindulgence. References to the Machine-Age modernism, a popular term of the time, were abundant: automobile imagery, streamlining, and much shiny metal, the material of airplanes. At the Empire State Building, the top seventeen-floor section of the 102-story tower purported to serve as a "mooring mast" for dirigibles, though it was never successfully used.

Unprecedented height and size were also expressions of modernity. Conceived in the last months of the stock market boom of the 1920s, and constructed as the economy slid into the Depression, the Empire State Building was two hundred feet taller than the Chrysler Building. More impressive, with 2.1 million square feet of floor space, it had more than twice the gross area of the Chrysler Building or of any other skyscraper of the time, except for the RCA Building at Rockefeller Center. And then there was its speed of construction: less than thirteen months after the first steel columns were set in April 1930, opening ceremonies were held on May 1, 1931 and the Empire State was ready to rent. At the peak of construction, the tower rose more than a story a day and 3,500 workers were employed on the site. No project has since matched that record.

Modern methods versus modern motifs—the question of a style that married those differences was not resolved when the Depression and World War II interrupted most development for more than a decade. When building resumed in the late 1940s, the basic factors that affect design had all changed: technology, materials, style, theory. Advances in technology, inside and out, made possible new architectural forms. Air conditioning and fluorescent light freed facades and floor plans from their traditional dependence on operable windows for ventilation and on the lightwells or courts that carved into the building mass. Stronger structural steel and welding rather than riveting made the frame more rigid and lighter. Improvements in plate glass as a curtain-wall material and a change in the city's building code to allow glass facades produced the most dramatic change. The U.N. Secretariat Building was the prototype for the slab solution to the high-rise form, an utterly simple rectangular box, with its broad expanse of east- and west-facing sides stretched over with a grid of tinted glass, a transparent plane that revealed the interior volume. Another pioneer of plate glass was Lever House, the exquisite emerald of Park Avenue, which turned the slender slab perpendicular to the street and lifted it above the sidewalk on *piloti* to emphasize the weightless volume of space within. In the Seagram Building across the avenue, uniform bays of brown tinted glass were separated by thin I-beam elements coated with bronze, the only ornament, in effect, on the facade. The "less is more" minimalism of German émigré Mies van der Rohe and the much-admired Seagram Building set the standard for skyscraper design of the 1960s, even if the progeny often did look, as the quip goes, "like the box the Seagram Building came in."

If New York architecture of the first half of the twentieth century favored an aesthetic of monumental mass, richly modeled surfaces, and lavish ornament, then the values from mid-century were the opposite—an emphasis on volume, plane, and transparency. In the decades after World War II, New York architecture embraced International Style modernism in theory and practice, as did most of American architectural culture, from the professional schools and magazines to corporate board rooms and government clients. Simply as a style, capital-M Modernism can be described by various characteristics that include an emphasis on modern materials, especially glass and metal; a taste for simple geometric forms—rectangles, grids, prisms, circles; the treatment of walls as planes or membranes, rather than as supporting elements or as surfaces for decoration; an emphasis on universal space and the open plan for interiors; and an appreciation of materials for their intrinsic qualities of color, texture, or pattern. Lever House and the Seagram Building are classics of the International Style on a corporate expense account. In both, the glass box was both a precious object and a transparent volume of offices, which, especially when seen illuminated from within at twilight and at night, made the interior world the architectural subject.

Glass has been both the brick and the limestone of the later twentieth century. It can be ordinary or exquisite. Used simply as a skin of great or little beauty, its quality of reflectivity can be manipulated with a formal and decorative effect. In the mid-1980s, the Fifth Avenue Trump Tower and the Jacob K. Javits Convention Center created simple envelopes of tinted glass, cut at corners with cubic and crystalline effects. At the Convention Center, from the exterior the vast expanses of glass are gridded with the geometry of the structure, while from the interior the membrane seems to disappear behind the diagonal tectonics of the frame and the stupendous space enclosed. In the late 1990s, French architect Christian de Portzamparc took a postmodern attitude to the glass box in the LVMH Building on Fifty-seventh Street, which used glass in a palette of tinted and translucent effects, as if creasing and folding the facade planes. The squeeze-play of this little mid-block tower makes a witty commentary on the lack of breathing space for architecture on midtown's pricey property.

Space is the ultimate luxury in New York. Rare indeed are the vast interior rooms on the scale of the Grand Central concourse, the open center of Frank Lloyd Wright's concrete spiral at the Guggenheim Museum, or the great outdoor room formed by the three theaters of Lincoln Center, framing its stage-set plaza and fountain. In the relentlessly commercial equation of Manhattan real estate, the square-foot value of space is based on the potential to multiply the full ground plot another floor every ten to fifteen vertical feet: monumental open space forfeits revenue into the future. Most New Yorkers understand a conspicuous display of empty space as both extravagance and a statement of high-style design, whether it is the minimalism of an ultra-chic Madison Avenue boutique or the expansive travertine plaza that distances the front door of the Seagram Building from the public sidewalk. Mies van der Rohe separated his skyscraper from the activity of the avenue, setting it back a full ninety feet to give the tower the presence of a discrete object in its own precinct. Earlier, at Rockefeller Center, Raymond Hood and the Associated Architects conceived the pedestrian paths through the complex—especially the Channel Gardens from Fifth Avenue to the sunken ice rink and the extra north-south street that formed a mid-block plaza—as a way to create an area that seemed more elite and expensive than the surrounding district.

Such space-making architecture is uncommon in Manhattan, and when it is accomplished, it is usually an expression of great wealth, will, or talent. In creating the Guggenheim and the Seagram Building, as architects of genius, Wright and Mies worked with exceptionally rich and receptive patrons. Hood applied his business acumen brilliantly to convince his client that additional open space would return higher rents throughout the complex. At the United Nations, the purchase and donation of a large parcel of land by John D. Rockefeller, Jr. provided an open area for a definitive statement of the International Style by a committee of architects led by Le Corbusier. At Lincoln Center, the will of the "Power Broker" Robert Moses met, again, the philanthropy of Rockefeller to raze the slum and to erect an art acropolis. There are, of course, many other fine examples in the city of "architecture in the round"—our nineteenth-century City Hall, Trinity Church, the U.S. Custom House, the New York Public Library and Bryant Park, the campus plan of Columbia University, among others. But architecture in open space is not the normal condition of New York—rather, it is contiguity. Most buildings form part of a street wall of fully built-up blocks, contiguous facades that touch and blend into an urban collage. Even the Chrysler Building and Empire State engage their neighbors on their mid-block sides. At their upper levels, of course, the towers are spectacular space markers, not space makers—unless one sees the skyline as the supreme expression of spatial composition.

New York has historically been a city of grand gestures and of sweeping plans that have organized immense areas of land or systems of infrastructure—for example, the 1811 Commissioners' Plan, the Croton Water System, Central Park, Brooklyn Bridge, the subway system, Grand Central and Park Avenue, and the twentieth-century bridges and tunnels. New York's skyscrapers, of course, stretched for records: at the turn of the century, there was the Ivins Syndicate Building at 15 Park Row; then in quick succession from 1907 to 1913, the Singer Building, Metropolitan Life Tower, and Woolworth Building; in the late 1920s, there were the Chrysler Building and Empire State; and in the early 1970s, the World Trade Center. Oddly, though, for the most part, these exceptionally ambitious projects were created by almost anonymous figures. Save for the Roeblings, Olmsted, and perhaps Gilbert, the authors of our most brilliant constructions have been conceived and executed by men whose names are not well known. The commercial architects of the skyscraper giants, though highly successful in their day, are not as famous as their signature buildings. Ironically, New York, which has been a city of celebrities in most fields of culture, has produced no resident architectural geniuses of the first rank such as Wright, Mies, or Le Corbusier, and the closest it has had to an enduring brand-name firm is McKim, Mead, and White.

Perhaps this is because the true genius of New York architecture lies in the city itself—the *genius loci*, the spirit of the place. The density, diversity, the continuous commotion of building and rebuilding—those conditions tend to drown out individual architectural gestures, unless they are the size of Central Park, the Empire State, or, alas, the Twin Towers. But the scale of those undertakings demands a committee of professions to plan and an army to execute. The magnificence of Manhattan comes from unrelenting ambition, competition, and cumulative effect—an endless collage. A history of New York architecture is a daunting proposition, but an appreciation of New York *as* architecture is as simple as turning the pages of this book.

New York Architecture

The Puck Building : 1886

295–309 Lafayette Street

Albert Wagner

In the early decades of the nineteenth century, developments in transportation, communication, and construction triggered the city's transformation from a low-rise, industrial port town to a thriving, monument-strewn, skyward-reaching financial and cultural capital. Completed in 1886 to house the printing facilities for *Puck*, a popular satirical magazine, the Puck Building was one of the last industrial structures to be built in New York during the last quarter of the nineteenth century.

Puck was named after the character from Shakespeare's *A Midsummer Night's Dream*. Cherubic sculptures representing that mischievous namesake remain today—one above the current main entrance on Lafayette Street and the other on the corner of Mulberry and Houston Streets, above the site of the building's original entrance—vestiges of the original occupant, imparting much of the building's considerable charm.

The building was designed by Albert Wagner, a German-born architect of notable success in New York City during the last quarter of the nine-

OPPOSITE: A statue of Puck by sculptor Henry Baerer stands above what was once the main entrance of the building that bears his name. OVERLEAF: Stacked rows of round-arched windows of decreasing scale are at the root of the Puck Building's distinctive character.

teenth century. Little is known of Wagner's history other than that he studied under Leopold Eidlitz, who was a noted practitioner of a mid- nineteenth-century German variation on Romantic Classicism known as *Rundbogenstil*, which roughly translates to "round-arched style." Not surprisingly, Wagner's association with Eidlitz is often credited as the source for the version of the Romanesque Revival style used for the Puck Building.

In the 1890s the building underwent two major renovations: the first added a nine-story addition to the south; the second truncated the building to the west to allow for the northward extension of Elm Place (now Lafayette Street) and the relocation of the main entrance from the Mulberry-Houston corner to the western facade. Wagner oversaw his building through both of these changes, ensuring the structure's adherence to his original aesthetic intentions.

Despite the building's conversion into highly coveted loft spaces, the structure appears much the same as it did more than a century ago. With its characteristic arched windows, its carefully articulated textures and patterns (which are created by the manipulation of the brick form itself, not separately cast or carved), and its rich orange color, the structure is a late nineteenth-century showpiece.

OPPOSITE: The Puck Building's southern facade, which faces the narrow service alley known as Jersey Street, was not treated in the rich, majestic manner of the more public facades, but it maintains a picturesque, consequential appeal of its own.

Grant's Tomb : 1897

Riverside Drive at West 122nd Street

John H. Duncan

When Ulysses S. Grant, the eighteenth president, died in the summer of 1885, the United States, twenty years after the resolution of the Civil War, was still striving to construct a solid foundation for its newfound unity. Per Grant's request, plans were immediately set in place for him to be buried in New York City, where he had spent much of the rather hapless last decade of his life. The civic leaders who organized the 1888 architectural competition for Grant's tomb wanted not only to commemorate the life of a former president and Civil War hero, but also to symbolically assert the stability and strength of the country that he had fought to unify. Though the first competition jury was unable to select a winner, the members of a second jury deemed the design of John H. Duncan, also known for his Soldiers' and Sailors' Memorial Arch in Grand Army Plaza, Brooklyn, to be the most fitting.

The design of the exterior was closely fashioned after Napoleon's tomb and the common interpretation of the famous Mausoleum of Halicarnassus

OPPOSITE: The form of Grant's Tomb—a massive block surmounted by a colonnaded rotunda—owes much to the supposed design of the fabled Mausoleum of Halicarnassus. **OVERLEAF**: Exterior view of rotunda with Grant's famous words "Let Us Have Peace" set high above the main entrance

The deeply coffered barrel vaults and dome of the tomb's interior. A mosaic at bottom center depicts General Robert E. Lee surrendering to Grant at Appomattox Court House in 1865.

(also Halikarnassos), one of the Seven Wonders of the Classical World. Situated on a rise, high above the Hudson River, the tomb was designed with four virtually identical facades, which cast a unified impression of mass, strength, and durability for miles in every direction. Today, having been eclipsed by development and further obscured by vegetation, much of the structure's original exterior purpose has been lost. The former unity of the facades that presented an equally impressive edifice in every direction has been replaced by a strong hierarchy, in which the only readily visible façade—that of the main entrance—is privileged with a processional path that cuts through the dense trees surrounding the structure. It is no longer a looming beacon of America's resounding strength and its victory over its own fissures, but a lovely monument in a park, visible to only the few who chance by it in this distant corner of Manhattan and the very few more who specifically seek it out.

The interior, however, remains much as it was, expressing the same sentiments that it did upon the day of its dedication in 1897. The simple and dignified twin sarcophagi of Grant and his wife, Julia, submerged in the central crypt of the main interior, serve as a somber reminder of the inevitability of death. Mosaics depict the deeds of the hero, raised to the height of myth along the outer walls. Finally the levels of reality below begin to dissolve ethereally as walls give way to deeply coffered barrel vaults yielding in turn to the creamy light of the rotunda high above our heads. It is at once an homage to one all-but-forgotten national hero and an allegorical expression of the journey of the human spirit.

Encapsulated in Grant's Tomb is a very simple story relating the complexity of the architectural dichotomy, its mutability and timelessness, to those same qualities of the human condition.

Bayard-Condict Building : 1899

65 Bleecker Street
Louis Sullivan with Lyndon P. Smith

W hen the United Loan and Investment Company commissioned
Louis Sullivan, in collaboration with the little-known New York
architect Lyndon P. Smith, to design its new twelve-story Bayard Building in
1897, Sullivan was well established as one of Chicago's premier architects.
Along with William Le Baron Jenny and Daniel H. Burnham (Flatiron
Building, 1902), he had developed architectural theories that we now know
as the Chicago school. In his work and his writing he promoted honest,
practical design in a field that had been thrown off balance by the advent of
such technological advancements as the elevator and the structural steel
frame, which suddenly allowed buildings to grow taller and larger than
ever before. Predominantly applied to commercial structures, an ideal
Sullivan facade would express (rather than obscure) the building's structural logic of steel cagework, while differentiating the functional layers
within the building into roughly three zones—commercial, office, and
cap—which Sullivan himself likened to the organization of a column with

OPPOSITE: The gridwork of the Bayard-Condict Building's underlying structure of
columns and slab floors is clearly expressed on its facade, despite its applied ornament. OVERLEAF: Sullivan's angels reconcile the strong vertical gesture of the pilas-
ters that cloak the underlying steel columns with the heavy horizontal cornice.

base, shaft, and capital. Despite Sullivan's rigorous attention to this very rational system, his theories did not preclude the use of ornament, nor did they overlook the importance of aesthetics beyond structural expression.

Though a handful of New York buildings from this period were clearly influenced by the Chicago School, the Bayard-Condict Building, Sullivan's only New York commission, stands as a singular expression of his ideology in the city. Its facade reveals Sullivan's dedication to the building's structural underpinnings; steel structural columns are expressed by the long, uninterrupted bands of light terracotta, and the horizontal planes of each floor are clearly defined by the rigidly repeating courses of ornate terracotta panels. At a basic level, the overall composition of the facade, created by uninterrupted vertical members that balance the bulk of horizontal members, is a faithful interpretation of the internal structure. At the same time, the facade also expresses the building's functional layers: with the two commercial stories at the base being differentiated from the middle—an elegant ten-story repetition of windows and detailed ornamental panels, unified by the vertical members that harken back to the fluting on an Ionic column—and the cap with its course of winged angels and heavy cornice clearly defining the structure's terminus.

Though Sullivan's eloquent modern, American ideology would soon be overwhelmed by the antiquarian, Old World–inspired Beaux-Arts wave, it would resurface some fifty years later as an inspiration for the Modern movement.

OPPOSITE: Detail view of ornamentation

Cooper-Hewitt, National Design Museum : 1902

2 East 91st Street

Babb, Cook & Willard

In the latter part of the nineteenth century, many of New York's elite families settled along Fifth Avenue to get as far away as possible from the unpleasantries of the island's gritty docks and industrial shores. In 1899, when Andrew Carnegie commissioned the firm of Babb, Cook & Willard to design his new home on Fifth Avenue, he would follow this trend, firmly establishing the section of Fifth Avenue along Central Park as an ideal location for the elite to settle. Here, just a few miles north of the city's center, he was able to escape the density and commotion of downtown, while maintaining a close enough proximity to be able to actively oversee his philanthropic interests, which included the funding of several libraries (in the city and elsewhere) and the hall of music that still bears his name. Though a scattering of mansions and other structures (most notably the Metropolitan Museum of Art) had already begun to rise in this area before Carnegie decided to build his mansion, many more would appear in the ensuing decades as more and more wealthy New Yorkers, among them

OPPOSITE: Art nouveau porte cochere at main entrance **OVERLEAF:** A view of the south facade from Carnegie's beloved family garden, now the Cooper Hewitt's sculpture garden

Glass and steel conservatory skylight

Otto Kahn and Henry Clay Frick, grew weary of the noise and congestion of downtown.

Satisfying Carnegie's request for a spacious yet modest structure, Babb, Cook & Willard appropriately applied a Georgian manor style, the restrained aesthetic of the Anglo-Saxon country manor (a style that also referenced Carnegie's Scottish heritage), rather than the ornate French and Italianate styles that were common among Fifth Avenue mansions.

In the end, however, Carnegie's mansion was a building of incomparable technological distinction and dignified grandeur. It was the first residential structure to utilize a steel structural frame, and one of the first single-family residences with an elevator. The interior temperature was maintained by a heating and cooling system that few buildings, residential or otherwise, had at the time. And the scattering of embellishments including the ornate Art Nouveau porte cochere (awning) at the main entrance and an elaborate glass and steel conservatory, proved that, despite any general stylistic austerity, this was the home of one of America's most powerful and wealthy men.

After Carnegie's death in 1919, his wife bequeathed the building to the Carnegie Corporation—a philanthropic organization established by Carnegie himself in to promote "the advancement and diffusion of knowledge and understanding"—which turned the property over to the Smithsonian Institution in 1972. The mansion was adapted in 1976 by Hardy, Holzman and Pfeiffer Associates to be the home of the Smithsonian's Cooper-Hewitt, National Design Museum, but much of the character of the original structure remains; only now, thanks to the Museum, its restrained grandeur and lovely garden can be enjoyed by all, a fate of which the philanthropic Carnegie would no doubt have approved.

Flatiron Building : 1902

175 Fifth Avenue

Daniel H. Burnham & Co.

Throughout the years, many people have believed that the Flatiron was something more than an oddly shaped tall office building, endowing the captivating structure with something of a mythical history. Contrary to popular belief, however, it was never the tallest building, nor was it the first skyscraper in New York. It was, at its opening, the northern-most structure of such note in Manhattan, and its wild popularity undoubtedly motivated for the trend toward tall office building construction in this area and beyond, making Madison Square an important stop on the north-bound journey of the city's center.

Designed by the Chicago-based architectural firm Daniel H. Burnham & Co., the Flatiron (originally known as the Fuller Building) was to house the offices of the George A. Fuller Company, America's largest construction company, and the contractor with whom Burnham brought a number of early Chicago School skyscrapers to fruition (see also, the Bayard-Condict Building).

OPPOSITE: A precarious-looking Flatiron Building towers between the diverging chasms of Broadway and Fifth Avenue. OVERLEAF, LEFT: The Flatiron Building from the intersection of Fifth Avenue and Broadway, at Madison Square Park. OVERLEAF, RIGHT: A decorative terracotta medallion

Given the limits of the wedge-shaped site at the intersection of Broadway and Fifth Avenue below Twenty-third Street, the architect had little choice as to the shape of his tower. And it is this incidental shape that has made the structure such an enduring favorite of New Yorkers and visitors alike. It gives the building its shifting formal quality: appearing like a dangerously narrow tower at acute angles, a curiously thin extrusion from slightly more oblique angles, and a sturdy wide block from the sides. (The shape, which gave the building its descriptive moniker, also creates the irregular windcurrents that have notoriously lifted many a respectable woman's skirts in the past century.) It would not be fair to say, however, that the designer played no role in the formation of this persistent icon. The repetition of floors virtually identical to the cornice provides a dizzying unity to the facade that streamlines the building and accentuates its height. Slightly undulating facades subtly enhance this vertiginous quality, making it difficult to maintain a sense of the structure's actual height. And the light terracotta cladding imparts a mystical quality, conjuring something of the form of an ivory tower in a fairytale—an image that has been trapped by the shutters of countless cameras since the Flatiron's completion.

U.S. Custom House : 1907

1 Bowling Green

Cass Gilbert

I n 1899 a competition was announced for the design of the new U.S. Custom House, a significant structure in the country's greatest port city. After two rounds of deliberation the jury chose the design of a newcomer to New York City, Cass Gilbert. Years earlier at MIT (the first American school of architecture), Gilbert had studied design theories recently imported from the renowned French Beaux-Arts ("Fine Arts") Academy by a number of American architects who had studied there. These theories, the body of which became known in America simply as Beaux Arts, relied heavily on the application of classical European styles. Beaux-Arts buildings were often envisioned as grand sculptures in and of themselves, formed on the basis of their main facade and plan, and the structures often tended toward the monumental. Gilbert's competition entry epitomized all the elements of a finely detailed Beaux-Arts structure befitting such a symbolically impor- tant civic structure as the Custom House. The jury's choice launched the meteoric New York career of a little-known Minnesotan who went on to

OVERLEAF: Anthropomorphic representations of North America (left) and Europe (right) flank the monumental entrance to the U.S. Custom House.
OVERLEAF #2: View of secondary facade

play a central role in an architectural movement that would change the face of New York forever: the skyscraper craze.

Taking advantage of the prominent site at the divergence of Broadway at Bowling Green, the building's entry facade, the focal point, faced the financial district and the flow of southbound traffic before it branched off on either side of the structure. This orientation created a processional for the passerby (one must first approach and behold before walking past the structure) and axis to the structure, both of which deliberately evoked a temple or monument, not just a federal administrative building.

By applying Classical and contemporary French styles to the structure, Gilbert further enhanced its monumentality while providing a noble backdrop for the rich allegorical sculpture that amply adorns the facade. The most striking sculptural elements are the four large sculptures of the Continents arranged along the front, which were designed by Daniel Chester French, one of the most sought-after artists of the time. At far left is Asia with the lotus flower and enslaved supplicants at her feet; then comes North America, enfolding the working man with her robe, and the winged wheel of Mercury, symbol of commerce, at her feet. Next is wise old Europe with a monk peering over her shoulder and a book in her lap, and finally, the sleeping embodiment of the African continent surrounded by the civic triumphs of her distant past. Together, at the entrance of this monument to commerce and prosperity, the sculptures elegantly express the American worldview at the time, the very worldview that had given rise to such a grandiose shell for this administrative structure.

Alwyn Court : 1908

180 West 58th Street

Harde & Short

Built between 1907 and 1908, the Alwyn Court apartment building stands as a reminder of a significant turn in the history of New York's development. As the city's population steadily grew after the close of the Civil War, then exploded with the great immigration, Manhattan's island boundaries became ever more apparent. As land prices began to reflect these restrictions, it was no longer practical or even possible for every wealthy figure in New York to stake a claim for his or her very own single-family mansion. And for many of those who could still afford single-family row houses, the limitations of the twenty-five-feet-wide-by-one-hundred-feet-deep lot regulated by the city's grid made quarters tight, dark and stagnant.

The upper and middle classes had long been contemptuous of apartment living. Not only did they frown upon the idea of *renting* a space rather than *owning* their own home, but they considered apartment living a lascivious institution whereby guests were entertained within view of the boudoir, befitting only the lower classes and the immoral French (who had

OVERLEAF: Artist Richard Haas's trompe l'oeil mural transformed this once dark and cramped airshaft into a bright, whimsical courtyard.

long ago accepted the apartment as a viable residential form). However, by the end of the nineteenth century, the majority of middle-class families had faced the new reality and either moved to the more spacious new boroughs or conceded to move into apartment buildings. Not long after, the refinements of apartment types would lure the rich out of their single-family homes into luxury apartment buildings, which, by virtue of their economy of space (building upward and housing several families on one small site), allowed families to enjoy all the pleasures of the houses that they left behind (often more) for a fraction of the cost.

Designed by the architecture firm of Harde & Short, Alwyn Court (named after one of its original owners, Alwyn Ball, Jr.) was one of the first luxury apartment buildings to go up in the quickly growing cultural district just south of Central Park, home, most notably, to Carnegie Hall. Though its drab internal airshaft roughly resembled that of a tenement, there was little else about the building that was comparable to that typical form of housing for the lower classes. The facades nearly dripped with molded terracotta embellishment: crowns and salamanders (symbols of the sixteenth-century French king Francois I, supporter of the 1524 expedition of Luigi da Verrazano who discovered New York Harbor) mingle with vines and cherubs to create an appearance of nearly overpowering extravagance. Each of the original twenty-two apartments contained fourteen rooms, which included five bathrooms, servants' quarters, and a formal reception gallery. Special closets were provided for storing gowns, while others were for hats, and each suite was provided with its very own wine vault.

OPPOSITE: The crowned salamanders symbolic of Francois I nestle above the original main entrance of the building (now the entrance to the genteel Petrossian Café).

ALWYN COURT APARTMENTS

This richly ornamented apartment house, built in 1907
-1909, is unique in the city. The architects, Harde & Short,
took full advantage of the economies of terra cotta,
a material then much in vogue. A single mold could be
used time and again for casting clay blocks which
were later fired and glazed. The profusion of intricate
detail that covers the entire building is in the style
of Francis I, the great art patron of Renaissance
France. His personal symbol, a crowned salamander, is
prominently displayed.

Plaque provided by the New York Community Trust, 1973

Then, as the flush times of the first quarter of the twentieth century met with the pallor of the Depression, the viability of such grand living fell off rapidly. Many of New York's nouveau riche found themselves newly broke, and one by one, Alwyn Court's apartments fell empty. In 1936 the last tenant took his leave, rendering the building completely vacant.

Three years later a new owner reconfigured the floor plans to accommodate a total of seventy-five three-to-five room apartments, at a much more manageable rent and scale. The main entrance on the corner of Fifty-eighth Street and Seventh Avenue became the entrance for commercial space, and a new residential entrance was located in the more private Fifty-eighth Street facade. There, a new lobby was decorated in the then popular Art Deco style, a treatment rather unsympathetic to the building's French Renaissance flamboyance.

Despite these changes, however, by 1980 the building was due for a considerable makeover. The white terracotta had been all but completely obscured beneath decades of soot and grime, and the heating, cooling, and insulation systems had grown both ecologically and economically inefficient. The cooperative committee (the building had been turned into cooperative apartments in the 1970s) commissioned the firm Beyer Blinder Belle to oversee extensive renovations. Experts restored the facade to its former glory using delicate tools and special chemicals that, in some cases, were created specifically for Alwyn Court. The Art Deco lobby was completely refurbished and decorated in a style better suited to the rest of the building. Windows were replaced, and mechanical systems were updated.

OPPOSITE: A commemorative lantern and historical plaque grace one of the more subdued planes of the Alwyn Court facade.

And in the most dramatic undertaking, the gloomy airshaft was converted to a warm, glowing atrium adorned with a trompe l'oeil architectural mural (created by Richard Haas) that playfully echoed the ostentation of the building's exterior treatment.

This careful restoration served to enhance the reputation of Beyer Blinder Belle as preservationists, a status that would soon lead them to two of New York City's most renowned restoration projects: Ellis Island and Grand Central Terminal.

OPPOSITE: Detail of exterior ornament with the fleur-de-lis—a French monarchical symbol—figuring heavily into the motif

Queensboro Bridge : 1909

East 59th-60th Street
Gustav Lindenthal and
Henry Hornbostel

When construction on the Queensboro Bridge began in 1901 under the direction of engineer Gustav Lindenthal and architect Henry Hornbostel, the idea of building a bridge that would finally link Manhattan and Queens was far from new. Discussion had begun as far back as the 1870s, when Queens was little more than farm country, but the matter became more pressing after the great incorporation of 1898 joined the five boroughs into one giant metropolis. At this point linkage between Manhattan and the city's outer boroughs was no longer a good idea, it was a mandate.

The primary design for a massive cantilevered structure had been put forth by the engineer R. S. Buck in 1899. Though Lindenthal would add a second road deck to the original plan, he would carry through the design much as it had been envisioned by Buck. Breaking from the suspension bridge tradition that had begun with the Brooklyn Bridge more than twenty years before, the cantilever structural plan creates the bridge's unique

OPPOSITE: A spiky decorative finial atop the Queensboro Bridge
OVERLEAF: The elegant industrial silhouette of the Queensboro Bridge at sunrise
OVERLEAF #2: Massive cantilevers coupled with a network of steel trusses act as primary support for this, the first bridge to link Manhattan and Queens.

appearance. Elegantly zigzagging trusses replaced swooping cables, supports were built at a considerably more delicate scale, and the size of the anchorage at either end was significantly diminished.

Hornbostel would, for his part, pay close attention to aesthetic details, overseeing everything from the pattern of the rivets and the spiky steel finials to the beautifully detailed Manhattan-side entry ramp with its sweeping granite expanses, delicately colored tile insets, and herringbone tile vaults created by the famed Guastavino family. The result is a delicately balanced composition of classical Beaux-Arts detail set against the industrial elegance of the innovative bridge structure itself—a breathtaking homage to the American Renaissance period during which it was created.

A renovation completed in 2000 restored decaying structural and ornamental members, retrofitted existing spaces for the inclusion of a dramatically vaulted grocery store and restaurant below the bridge's Manhattan entrance ramp, and created a neighboring modern structure that houses a household goods design shop. With these changes, the bridge that was intended to sew the disparate parts of the metropolis together has been stitched into the urban fabric itself, a more truly integrated member of the city's form than perhaps any other such structure in New York.

Grand Central Terminal : 1913

42nd Street and Park Avenue

Warren & Wetmore, Reed & Stem

In 1854, complaints concerning the noise and filth produced by steam-powered locomotives forced Cornelius Vanderbilt—the New York Central Railroad baron once rumored to be the richest man in the world—to relocate his terminal rail station from Thirty-second Street and Fourth Avenue to Forty-second Street, which at the time was on the fringe of the commercial city. Using various powers of persuasion, Vanderbilt soon came to an agreement with the city whereby in return for allowing him to disrupt the street grid with a new station at the intersection of 42nd Street and 4th Avenue, he would provide a compensatory street along the western facade of his new structure, which in effect provided little more than a dead-end accessway for loading and unloading goods and passengers from his very own station.

The northward move of the railroad had allayed the problem of direct contact between the city's residential centers and the pollution that the engines created, but other problems of steam power still remained. Because steam locomotives could not travel in tunnels (the trapped smoke and soot would have asphyxiated passengers) the railroad's tracks were bridged with an open lattice of streets for several blocks to the north of the station's rail yard, thus allowing smoke to escape through the holes between street beds.

Though this solution maintained the city's grid, established a useful connection between the areas on either side of the tracks north of Forty-second Street, and helped, to a limited extent, to curb noise and smoke, the areas directly to either side of the tracks remained largely undeveloped. When a 1902 collision in the cut below the gridwork killed seventeen people by asphyxiation, the railroad could no longer ignore the necessity for a cleaner, safer method of locomotion.

In 1905, after the trains had been fully electrified, the holes to the north were covered, and excavation began for new submerged tracks and a new station that would proclaim the momentous shift in technology, transportation, and indeed, daily life in New York and the rest of the world. In this station, the railroad's brilliant chief engineer, William Wilgus, had envisioned not just a space where passengers would come and go on trains, but a multifunctional, fully integrated urban gateway where commuters could get a shoe shine, make connections to the IRT's new Fourth Avenue subway line, grab a bite to eat, do a little shopping, and enjoy the most modern conveniences in baggage handling and ticketing. Wilgus, fully aware of the costly nature of such an undertaking, recognized that the Railroad could sell off the use of the area above the newly enclosed tracks to developers for a considerable profit. Thus Wilgus pioneered the idea of "air rights," sparking the rapid development of the area to the north and ensuring the financing for the new station.

With the experienced rail station architects Reed & Stem overseeing the spatial arrangement of the various programs and the fashionable young

PREVIOUS SPREAD: The recently renovated Main Concourse forms the heart of the city's commuter hub. OPPOSITE: Mercury sits atop the terminal's main (south) facade as the Chrysler Building and the Grand Hyatt Hotel loom beyond.

Beaux-Arts firm of Warren & Wetmore seeing to the overall aesthetics, the station slowly took form.

Though construction was not quite complete, the station officially opened in 1913 to rave reviews. The formidable facades were punctured with tall arched windows reminiscent of the triumphal arches of Rome. The sixteen-foot-tall sculpture that crowns the pediment, proclaiming the presence of the structure for several blocks down Park Avenue, was fashioned by French sculptor Jules Alexis Coutan and depicts the figures of Minerva, goddess of wisdom and skill; Mercury, god of transportation and commerce; and Hercules, a mythical hero representing strength and endurance. Together with myriad other finely crafted, attentively scaled Beaux-Arts details, these elements created the visage of an impressive urban monument celebrating the thriving city and the clean and efficient transportation system that would only augment its prosperity and growing importance.

Inside, Wilgus's vision was carried through nearly to the letter. An efficient network of tunnels, passageways, and stairwells connected a dining concourse with shopping areas, tracks with subways, and everything in between, all amidst the glow of polished marble surfaces. Crisply stenciled black signs were highly visible on the pale marble, guiding passengers along their way, and illuminated, marquis-style boxes clearly announced the locations of the various tracks; both enhanced the coherence of the carefully engineered system of connections.

Six years later, the completion of the Vanderbilt viaduct roadway would finally amend Cornelius Vanderbilt's incursion into the city's precious grid. It carries traffic up and around the station's central mass and lets it off onto Park Avenue (as Fourth Avenue had been renamed) in either direction.

In 1928, Warren & Wetmore completed the New York Central Building (now the Helmsley Building), a stout Beaux-Arts skyscraper that held railroad and other offices. From the south, the station building appeared as a monumental gateway base for this new structure. From the north, two tunnels allowing the viaduct traffic to pass dramatically through the new structure's base recapitulated the language of the monumental gateway for those approaching from the north. In that direction, Park Avenue had been rapidly developed with wealthy apartment buildings in the tradition of Alwyn Court since electrification had finally sent train traffic completely underground.

In the 1960s, as the railroad company gasped for life, its usefulness having been rapidly usurped over the previous decades by the growing ubiquity of the automobile and the airplane, the station was threatened with demolition. Desperate for salvation, the railroad set its sights on the lucrative prospect of high-rise development. In 1961 famed architect Walter Gropius's Pan Am Building (now Met Life Building) rose fifty-nine stories between the New York Central and Grand Central Terminal buildings, on the site of the station's old office and baggage claim structure. This building, while clearly a disruption in the dialogue between those two Beaux-Arts structures, maintained the viaduct circulatory path while creating valuable internal connection between the station and the streets to the north. It also generated much-needed revenue for the railroad.

In 1967, in an effort to protect the terminal building from further alteration or possible destruction, the incipient Landmarks Preservation Commission endowed the structure with official landmark status—a safeguard that proved useful in the very next year, when the profit-starved railroad initiated plans to build a fifty-story tower directly above Grand Central Terminal. For ten years a legal battle waged on between those who wished to

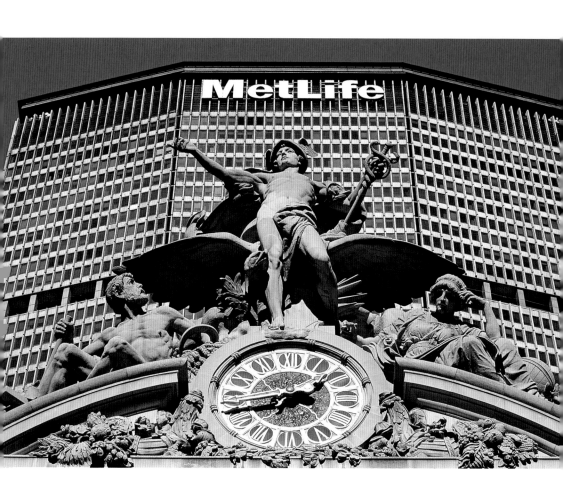

PREVIOUS SPREAD: Minerva looks on thoughtfully as the Grand Central clock registers the passing time. ABOVE: The MetLife building towers over Coutan's colossal sculptural group.

build and those who wished to preserve. In 1978 the latter emerged victorious when the Supreme Court handed down its decision to preserve the terminal.

By this time, however, the structure had fallen into serious disrepair. Once-gleaming interior walls were dull and drab. The ceiling mural—once a symbolic connection between the earthly glory of the station and that of the heavens above—had been obscured by the same soot and grime that encrusted the windows, blocking out precious light, and garish and hastily applied commercial displays plagued the great central space. With the fresh presence of the Metropolitan Transit Authority (MTA), which had taken over management of the station and its lines shortly after the Supreme Court's 1978 ruling, and the help of many of the people and organizations that had made the preservation of the structure's very existence possible, repairs and the funds needed to make them slowly came about. In 1988 the MTA, in a major move, selected the firm of Beyer Blinder Belle, whose careful restoration had returned Alwyn Court and the structures of Ellis Island to their original glories, to effect a major restoration and redevelopment plan. Over the next ten years, as work proceeded, sunlight began to shine through the once grimy windows, the massive Kodak billboard that had come to dominate the Main Concourse was removed, surfaces shone with new luster, and the rich celestial mural once again forced commuters to turn their eyes skyward. At the same time, a second grand stair was added directly across from the existing one, as had originally been intended, enhancing the grandeur and nearly perfect symmetry of the Main Concourse. New pedestrian linkages made circulation through the various concourses even easier than before.

Today the structure stands as a monument to the ingenuity of the integrated, multiuse plan, and the crowning glory of the preservation movement.

Woolworth Building : 1913

233 Broadway

Cass Gilbert

When Frank Woolworth approached Cass Gilbert (see also the U.S. Custom House) in 1910 to design the New York headquarters for his F. W. Woolworth & Co. variety store empire, corporate towers had already replaced church steeples as the most significant elements of the lower Manhattan skyline, and the very idea of the "skyline" as a significant part of a city's appearance was just taking form. The high-rise commercial building made possible with the advent of the structural steel frame and the elevator, offered not only a practical ideal—allowing optimum land usage and high levels of natural light—but also a highly visible, iconic, advertising architecture. Woolworth, who wanted the new headquarters to stand out from the rest, requested a tower modeled on the Gothic Victoria Tower of London's Houses of Parliament, in contrast to the French-mannered Singer Building (Ernest Flagg, 1908) nearby in lower Manhattan.

Gilbert had already experimented with the Gothic just a few blocks away on his 90 West Street Building in 1907. And for New York's evolving

OPPOSITE: Woolworth's gothic tower against an azure sky. **OVERLEAF:** The back-lit leaded glass panel in the lobby gives the impression of a skylight.

The vaulted ceiling of the lobby is encrusted with sparkling glass mosaics.

skyline, he foresaw a romantic composition of towers, much like those he had admired during his travels through medieval Flemish cities. With its lofty spikes, the Gothic had epitomized man's eternal quest to reach the heavens, and Gilbert considered it a perfect architectural expression for the rising city.

He began with a massive base, surmounted by a tower positioned at the center of the Broadway facade, much like a steeple over the entrance of a church. Long vertical lines at regular intervals along the facade visually lightened the mass of the base while uniting base and tower. A series of setbacks tapered the tower to its ornate culmination. Each setback was embellished with ornate tracery, including peaks and spikes, relentlessly negating the horizontal lines wrought by the setback. The overall composition was insistently vertical, ever oriented toward the sky.

Any ecclesiastical sensation invoked by the organization and detail of the exterior was heightened by the interior. The cruciform layout of the foyer echoes the typical floor plan of the Gothic cathedral, while glistening mosaics on the ceiling recall the extravagant material detail of Baroque churches (despite the mosaics' actual imagery, which is of the modern world of commerce).

"Cathedral of commerce," an epithet that the structure acquired soon after its completion in 1913, was keenly appropriate, not only because it was an office tower that looked resembled a colossal Gothic cathedral, but because of its power to inspire. It succeeded as a powerful symbol signaling the beginning of an architectural tide that would transform New York's

architectural, commercial, and psychological character forever. Just as intense spirituality had motivated medieval Europeans to thrust cathedral spires high into the heavens in an effort to assert ultimate spiritual dedication, so too would the spirit of capitalism inspire many modern businesses to puncture the sky with ever more fantastic towers, each one attempting to assert the superiority of one corporate identity over the others.

OPPOSITE: Gothic tracery at the crown of the tower   ABOVE: The church-like interior of the lobby

Consolidated Edison Company Building : 1926

4 Irving Place

Warren & Wetmore

The Consolidated Edison Company Building is not only a fine and oft overlooked member of New York's skyscraper family, but its intriguing architectural evolution is a manifestation of the ever-changing, adaptive character that makes the city unique. In 1910 the Consolidated Gas Company, which had occupied a few small, former residential buildings along Irving Place, commissioned the design and construction of a large annex for the quickly growing enterprise. But in just a few years, the company had already outgrown this structure, so Henry J. Hardenbergh, noted for his Dakota Apartments and Plaza Hotel, was commissioned to design a taller and wider new building that would integrate the existing structure, which was still in fine condition having been built so recently. But because this structure was not equipped to handle the bulk of the seven additional stories called for in the design, Hardenbergh and his engineers had to devise an ingenious structural method. It began with the construction of new masses on either side of the existing central building. At the roof level

OPPOSITE: The memorial cap of the Consolidated Edison Company Building

of that structure, girders were laid across to rest on the frames of the additions, forming a structural bridge above the existing mass, and from there, construction proceeded in a more traditional fashion.

In order to unify the disparate masses created by this unorthodox structural system, Hardenbergh maintained the existing facade and duplicated its rhythms and details across the surface of the new forms so every part blended into a unified whole that looked something like a large Italian Renaissance palazzo. By day, the building maintained the sort of indistinct quality of any number of large office structures in the city, but by night it became a dazzling gas company billboard with a distinctive illuminated sign on its roof and dramatically uplit facades that announced the identity of its owner and occupant.

About a decade later, the newly formed Consolidated Edison Company (a conglomerate of several smaller electric and gas companies) controlled most of the city's power supply, and it needed room to grow. The company secured the prestigious firm of Warren & Wetmore to oversee yet another expansion of the palazzo. This time, however, the intention was not to integrate new extensions, but to incorporate a dazzling new tower to rival that of the Metropolitan Life Insurance Company, just a few blocks north, as the crowning jewel of that era's midtown business district. The result was an expanded base that followed the stylistic precedent of the first twelve-story structure, surmounted by a stout, square tower that culminated in a torch-capped, Classical mausoleum-like form that served (at least nominally) as a monument to the Con Ed employees lost in World War I. As a cheerful,

would-be coincidence, this memorial detail was by night a glowing temple to the miracle of electricity—a stunning and highly visible advertisement for Con Ed's product.

Since the building's completion in 1926, many taller and architecturally more significant structures have been built, Con Ed's utter control of New York's power supply has rendered its need for advertisement moot, the lost soldiers memorialized by the tower's cap are all but forgotten, and the practice of illuminating corporate tower tops is as good as rote. And yet, somehow, perhaps as a result of its eclectic past, the Con Ed Building remains distinctive, as beautiful and charming from the observation deck of the Empire State Building as from the base of Bernard Rosenthal's cube at Astor Plaza.

OPPOSITE: The crowning torch built to commemorate the Con Ed employees lost to World War I; it also serves as a symbol of the company responsible for providing the majority of the city's electricity.

Hearst Building : 1928

951-969 8th Avenue

Joseph Urban and

George B. Post & Sons

The Hearst publishing legacy was founded in 1880, when George
Hearst acquired the *San Francisco Examiner* as compensation for a
gambling debt. In 1887 the *Examiner* was taken over by his son, the rather
spirited William Randolph Hearst, who turned the paper into one of the
West Coast's most popular (and sensational) journals. Eight years later,
William moved to New York City, where he acquired control of the *New
York Morning Journal*. Within a few years, he had parlayed his newspaper
resources into a number of magazines, and by the 1930s the Hearst enterprise had laid claim to no less than twenty newspapers, thirty magazines,
and several radio stations.

Along the way, Hearst had also acquired a taste for the glamour and
liveliness of the New York theater scene, which had crept northward at a
steady pace for decades. When he first settled on the vicinity of Columbus
Circle as the home of his magazine headquarters, he intended to develop the
area into the theater culture's prosperous new center. Over the next few

OPPOSITE: Theatrical figures grace the base of one of the torchlike columns
meant to introduce a tower that has yet to be built

decades, he bought land in the area at a dizzying rate, building hotels, funding the construction of Zeigfeld's glamorous new theater, and planning still more structures of a similar ilk. When the Metropolitan Opera Company found itself in search of new quarters and without considerable funds of its own, Hearst saw the ultimate opportunity to solidify his new cultural center.

Settling on the site bounded by Fifty-seventh and Fifty-eighth Streets along Eighth Avenue, which abutted the intended location for the new opera house, he hired his close friend Joseph Urban, the renowned Austrian theater designer who had once studied under the influential Otto Wagner, to design a tower that would serve as the focal point of his intended theater district. Because Urban had relatively little experience in designing large structures, Hearst had also retained the services of the noted commercial architects George B. Post & Sons. In 1927 construction began on the remarkable six-story tower base. The young German sculptor Henry Kreis created the structure's distinctive sculptural elements: simple, angular personifications of music, athletics, literature, and other humanities, with planar attributes that yield strong contrasts of light and shadow, imparting an air of drama to the facade as a whole.

The base was completed in 1928, by which time Hearst's unfettered speculation had brought financial burdens, and the Metropolitan Opera had abandoned its plan for a new home on Fifty-seventh Street. Consequently, Hearst halted further construction until his plans were back in order. However, with the Depression, Hearst's financial situation worsened, and in 1937 he was forced to turn his empire over to angry creditors.

OPPOSITE: Henry Kreis's anthropomorphic representations of music and war

In the years that followed, the base remained stunted, a memorial of the failed vision and ruinously excessive zeal of one of New York's most colorful personalities.

Now, after the better part of a century, the Hearst Publishing Company has commissioned the architect Sir Norman Foster, 1999 recipient of the Pritzker Prize for architectural excellence, to finally erect the tower Hearst had envisioned. Foster's faceted glass-and-steel lattice structure will rise forty-two stories from the center of the existing structure, playing the ethereal foil to Urban's heavy granite base and inserting its own character into the theatrical performance of light and shadow. With the tower's realization, the completion of the colossal new AOL/Time Warner headquarters at Columbus Circle, and the presence of the Trump International Hotel, the area just might play host to a bustling cultural/commercial center worthy of Hearst's dynamic vision.

OPPOSITE: A computer rendering of Sir Norman Foster's faceted glass-and-steel tower, rising above the existing limestone base

Chrysler Building : 1930

405 Lexington Avenue

William Van Alen

Completed in 1930, the Chrysler Building was one of the most signifi-cant marks on the skyward timeline since the completion of Cass Gilbert's iconic Woolworth Building in 1913. It is a building that, from drawing board to steely spire, epitomized the drama and fierce competition of the skyscraper race.

Walter P. Chrysler was a man of exceptional drive and ingenuity. Having risen through the ranks of the railroad industry, he moved into the automobile industry and became a key administrative figure, first with General Motors. He then moved on to mastermind the reorganization of the Willys-Overland Company and eventually became the head of the Maxwell Motor Company, which introduced the first car to bear his name in 1924. Incorporating such technological innovations as hydraulic breaks, the car was such a breakout success that within a year, he was able to change the company's name to the Chrysler Corporation. Within the next few years, the corporation would enjoy sky-rocketing success, inspiring

OPPOSITE: The Chrysler Building was the world's tallest building until the Empire State Building captured the distinction about one year after the Chrysler's glis-tening spire was raised. OVERLEAF: The unique illuminated "Vs" of the Chrysler Building's crown make it one of the most identifiable structures in New York.

Chrysler's decision to build his company's towering headquarters in Manhattan.

Though the appearance of the structure itself would have been enough to attract considerable attention at the time, architect William Van Alen's determination to build the tallest building in the world would cause a noteworthy sensation. First Van Alen dueled with J. E. R. Carpenter, winning when Carpenter reluctantly capped off his Lincoln Building at fifty-four stories. Then, in a far more animated battle, Van Alen faced his former partner, H. Craig Severence, a man from whom he had recently and unpleasantly parted, who was the architect for the new Bank of Manhattan Company Building at 40 Wall Street. During construction, workers kept daily tabs on the progress of their rival building, anxious to see who had come to the fore. As the buildings slowly rose, the two architects continued to revise their plans, adding floors and height-boosting crowns. Finally, when it appeared that Van Alen's creation was at last complete, Severence capped off his seventy-two-story structure and rejoiced in his victory. Days later, however, a spire roughly twelve stories high, which had been secretly constructed in the Chrysler Building's fire shaft, was raised up through the roof and bolted into place, making Van Alen the victor by a safe margin of over 200 feet.

Van Alen's intention, however, was to create not only the tallest building, but also the most impressive, the most beautiful, and the most *modern*—an architectural trophy for himself and a powerful symbol for his patron. Inside, simple, yet striking, metallic geometric designs, typical of

OPPOSITE: Decorative eagle gargoyles modeled after the hood ornaments of the 1929 Chrysler OVERLEAF, LEFT: Detail of the Chrysler Building's cap. The distinctive crescents were intended to resemble stacked hubcaps.

OVERLEAF, RIGHT: A lavishly detailed elevator door in the building's grand foyer

the Art Deco era, embellished elevator doors, railings, and floors. The ceiling of the main entry vestibule on Lexington Avenue was painted with a mural by Edward Trumbull, a well-known artist, that depicted aggrandizing scenes of commerce and industry with earnest, angular-jawed men toiling over powerful modern machines.

Outside, black-and-white bricks were arranged into showy patterns that added interest to the long tower shaft. Winged helmets, lotus flowers, and colossal versions of the aquiline Chrysler hood ornament glinted in the sun at each setback, showy tributes to the company's commercial and cultural importance. And the building's crowning glory—the glistening dome made out of stacked abstract forms of hubcaps—cast Chrysler's glory for miles around.

The Chrysler Building was boldly self-referential and unabashedly dramatic in its embellishments; it was, and is, in many ways, the crowning glory of the race that shaped the city.

PREVIOUS SPREAD: Details from Edward Trumbull's famous murals depicting strong men toiling to build the Chrysler Building OPPOSITE: A stylized lotus blossom finial adorns one of the building's setbacks.

Empire State Building : 1931

350 Fifth Avenue

Shreve, Lamb & Harmon

J ohn J. Raskob was a General Motors executive and one of the pioneers behind the installment plan method for buying automobiles, an innovation that not only revolutionized the auto industry but also played a role in developing the credit-based consumerism that characterizes our present economy. Just before the abrupt collapse of the thriving 1920s economy plunged both the American economy and the American psyche into a decade of depression, Raskob broke ground for his own special entry in the skyward contest, the Empire State Building. A principal investor in the project was Pierre S. du Pont, for whom Raskob was a personal secretary at the beginning of his career at General Motors, and former New York governor Alfred E. Smith served as president of the Empire State Company. Unlike the Woolworth and Chrysler Buildings, which were built with a mind toward corporate identity, this new enterprise was one of pure speculation and competitive spirit—a real-estate venture in which the investors hoped that drama and monumentality would prove sufficient incentive to bring tenants clamoring to fill its spacious floors.

OPPOSITE: The crown of the Empire State Building was first illuminated in 1964 on the occasion of the New York World's Fair.

Despite the economic disaster that occurred so shortly after construction began, Raskob pushed on, convinced that the slump was only temporary. The general contractors, Starrett Brothers & Eken, helped to organize the project and ensure that it ran smoothly, as one of the goals was to complete the building in time for annual leases to begin on May 1, 1931. The carpenters, ironworkers, and other skilled laborers employed in the building's construction worked quickly and steadily, closely adhering to the schedule. Although they knew that the sooner they finished, the sooner they would be out of work, the men were nonetheless thankful to stave off the fate of unemployment for even a little while longer. Thus, the building rose at an unprecedented rate. It had taken more than two years to raise the Chrysler Building to its 1,046-foot pinnacle just months before; all 1,252 feet of the Empire State Building would require only eleven months.

The building's architects, Shreve, Lamb & Harmon, had seen to it that style and utility were not sacrificed for speed of construction. Because the basic purpose of the building was to provide copious rentable space, principal designer William Lamb arranged the elevators into a tight core at the center of the building, where they would take up as little floor space as possible. As setbacks on the higher stories limited the floor space and therefore the number of people requiring access to these levels, so too would the number of elevators diminish, maximizing valuable square footage.

Despite many of Lamb's more practical concessions and his general aversion to unnecessary embellishment, he was certainly not blind to the pleasure and necessity of aesthetics, particularly in a building whose appearance acted

OPPOSITE: The Empire State Building acts as a familiar point of orientation for miles around. OVERLEAF, LEFT: From sidewalk to spire, the Empire State Building rises 1,250 feet—a length equivalent to that of nearly five city blocks. OVERLEAF, RIGHT: The Empire State Building dwarfs the Metropolitan Life Insurance Building (only half a mile to the south) as the twin towers loom in the distance.

as stimulus for renting its floor space. Long, clean metal ribs running vertically along the facades served to lighten the mass of the huge tower, carrying the eye skyward and further enhancing the building's considerable height. The setbacks, required by zoning, are unembellished and so minor compared to the structure's overall size that they barely interrupt the sweep of the facade until the observation deck at the base of the failed dirigible mooring post. (After two fairly unsuccessful attempts to use this structure as a docking station for dirigibles [zeppelins], the building's managing board conceded defeat to the strong winds that prevail at such heights. The mooring post is now recognized as the tower's impressive glowing lantern.) Though the main entry lobby on Fifth Avenue is more of a gesture than a necessity considering the arrangement of the circulation space, Lamb understood the lobby to be an important element that provided visitors with their first interior impression. The Empire State Building's lobby is in many ways a shrine to the building itself, with a gleaming Art Deco image of the building at the end of the large entry hall, underscored by its name and surrounded by shining starbursts, reminding visitors of the sleek, modern elegance of the structure they had just entered. Medallions along the glossy marble walls commemorate the hard work of the skilled laborers who made the building a reality, and the feats of engineering and construction that the building represents.

Though the long economic slump would leave Raskob's new masterpiece partially empty for nearly two decades, and the building would never quite succeed in living up to the financial predictions that Raskob had made, it achieved great success as an image, proudly marking the center of the ultimate metropolis.

OPPOSITE: The lantern of the Empire State Building, surmounted by the failed dirigible mooring post, which has found more useful employment as a radio tower

George Washington Bridge : 1931

West 181st Street

Othmar H. Ammann

The George Washington Bridge opened in 1931, holding the title of the longest suspension bridge in the world (nearly twice as long as any of its predecessors), as well as the first and only Hudson River bridge crossing between Manhattan and New Jersey. Though the bridge has long since lost the former, rather quantitative distinction, it remains to this day the only above-river direct connection between New Jersey and Manhattan. This fact is due in great measure to the brilliance and foresight of its engineer and designer, Swiss-born Othmar H. Ammann. No stranger to bridge design, Ammann had acted as right-hand man to the famed Gustav Lindenthal during construction of the dramatic, arch-support Hellgate railroad bridge over the East River in 1917 and assisted the same man again a few years later in creating a design proposal for a massive bridge connecting New Jersey and Manhattan at Fifty-seventh Street. It was customary at the time for engineers to design double-deck roadbeds with trusses in between to provide enough rigidity to withstand the stresses of wind and

OPPOSITE: Lit cables and streaming traffic accentuate the long, graceful lines of the bridge by night.

loading. Lindenthal had incorporated this solution into his Fifty-seventh Street bridge design, but due to its tremendous span (the distance across the Hudson is greater than across the East River) and to the massing necessary to anchor cables that could make such a construction work, the plan was rejected. When Ammann submitted his own design in 1924, he had discovered that girders placed across the roadbed would create enough strength for a single deck to withstand the inherent stresses; thus a thinner profile could be maintained, requiring less massive cables, supports, and anchorage. Ground was broken in 1927.

Though Ammann was first and foremost a brilliant bridge engineer inclined toward function and economy before all else, he maintained a strong aesthetic propensity. He had envisioned his completed George Washington Bridge as consisting of two solid Classical or Gothic supports—originally to be cloaked in poured concrete, later to be clad in granite sheathing—strung over with delicate cables and between by a thin strip of road. It was not to serve simply as a utilitarian bridge connecting two land masses but as a monumental gateway. However, before he could realize such an image, the Depression struck, and funding for the materials to cover the steel armatures was revoked. The supports were to remain bare. Ironically, the finished product was nothing of the Beaux-Arts masterpiece that its creator had intended, but it was heralded by such modernists as Le Corbusier for its elegant, honest simplicity.

Thirty-one years later, after a steady increase in automobile traffic, Ammann—who had also seen the Bayonne and Triborough bridges to com-

OPPOSITE: The structural lattice of the George Washington Bridge supports was once intended to be obscured beneath a granite sheath.

pletion in 1931 and 1936, respectively—was called in to design a second roadbed. Though his original plans had called for one slim roadbed to keep costs at a minimum, Ammann had foreseen just such an increase. He had designed the bridge to withstand more loading than was necessary for a single roadbed with the intention that another roadbed would be added when demand arose. Utilizing roughly the same method that he had for the first, he deftly fitted the bridge with a second thin roadbed suspended close beneath the first, maintaining the delicacy of the original profile.

In 2000 the lighting design firm Domingo Gonzalez Associates designed a lighting scheme that gave the bridge a nighttime presence (on special occasions, such as holidays), rivaling its already considerable day-time beauty. A series of powerful floodlights were planted within the steel lattice of the towers, lighting them from within with breathtaking effect: the two 604-foot-tall supports are transformed into glowing crystal filigree that reflect on the water below.

Group Health Insurance Building

(originally the McGraw-Hill Building) **:** 1931

330 West 42nd Street

Raymond Hood, Godley & Foulhoux

The McGraw-Hill publishing company in the late 1920s was in dire need of a new home. It had outgrown its headquarters and had departments and subsidiaries scattered all over the city. In 1929 a new building committee was formed to acquire a new site and oversee the design and construction of a building that would house the company and all of its constituencies—printing presses and editors alike. A zoning law that prohibited the establishment of printing plants between Third and Seventh Avenues ruled out the possibility of situating McGraw-Hill's new omnibuilding in the center of the city, so the committee began to search around the city's fringes.

In 1926 a real estate developer named John Larkin had proposed a sensational plan to build a 110-story tower of a bland, generically Art Deco style. During the three years preceding his proposal, Larkin had systematically acquired small plots between Forty-first and Forty-second Streets and Eighth and Ninth Avenues until he had amassed the impressive 47,500-

square-foot lot upon which he intended to build this enormous tower. Had the Larkin Tower been built, it would have been the tallest building in the world at the time, but this was never to be. In 1930, anxious to unload the undeveloped site, he offered a deal to the McGraw-Hill company that it was unable to refuse: its old, outsized headquarters for his massive building site.

Situated on Forty-second Street, a major thoroughfare across the city, it was right across the street from the IRT's new Eighth Avenue subway line and within a few blocks of the city's two major transportation hubs, Pennsylvania Station and Grand Central Terminal. Though the area surrounding the site—filled with flophouses, tenements, and less-than-reputable business establishments—was not ideal, the site would serve quite well enough.

Once the committee had found its site, the popular architect Raymond Hood was selected to design the new headquarters. Hood kept the arrangement of the building's functions in mind: commercial space with large glass fronts at street level, production space on the few higher-ceilinged floors above, rentable space above that, the company's office space where setbacks began, and an executive office suite on the top few floors after the final setback (with narrower floors that allow for more natural light). Yet Hood also had the foresight to make the plan of the building adaptable to whatever use its tenants might desire in the future. Thus, each floor is an open slab that can be configured as needed, with elevators and structure at the center. He provided copious natural light for workers by organizing windows in bands, interrupted only by the necessary supporting members,

OPPOSITE: The Art Deco profile of the Group Health Insurance Building from the east OVERLEAF: With its sleek lines and high-gloss finishes the renovated lobby entrance underscores the GHI Building's Art Deco character at the street level.

that stretched from a few inches above the floor to the ceiling (the maximum height the law would allow). By self-description Hood was a devoutly practical designer, never forgoing comfort, economy, or functionality for aesthetics, and in the McGraw-Hill Building, at just about every turn, this characterization seems to ring true, right down to the green wall paint that he said was the most relaxing color to the eye.

While all of these elements make the McGraw-Hill Building a structure of note, its most significant quality is that of marking an architectural turning point. The dramatic setbacks of the east-west silhouette tie the building to the Art Deco trend, but the strong presence of the nearly continuous horizontal window courses and the block-shaped north-south silhouette link the building with the distinctive International Style structures soon to come.

Though the building changed hands in 1974 when the McGraw-Hill Company established its new headquarters in the Rockefeller Center extension at 6th Avenue, aside from renovations to the lobby, the building has not been significantly altered since its completion.

The Cloisters : 1939

Fort Tryon Park

Allen, Collens & Willis

John D. Rockefeller, Jr., was a man known for his great wealth and power, but he was also a tremendous lover of art, music, and history, and a generous philanthropist. When the medieval sculptural and architectural collection of George Grey Barnard became available, Rockefeller donated a significant sum to the Metropolitan Museum of Art to ensure its purchase. The collection contained a number of remarkable artifacts, including nearly complete cloisters and chapels from medieval monasteries and the sarcophagi of Spanish noblemen. Rockefeller was not content for such objects to be placed inside glass cases in the Met's main building on Museum Mile, out of context and maintaining little more than a decorative purpose. He wanted the collection to be displayed in a more sensitive manner, where scholars, students, and laymen alike could appreciate the artifacts in a setting more reflective of the European homes from whence they came.

He purchased a high, rocky site where a Revolutionary War fort once stood. Far north of the distractions of lower Manhattan and overlooking the

The terracotta-tiled roofs and tower of the Cloisters rise above the trees of Fort Tryon Park.

Hudson and the undeveloped New Jersey Palisades, it was the most ideal setting he could have found on the island of Manhattan. Rockefeller donated this site to the city to be used for a park, stipulating that the four acres toward the northern extreme be set aside for the construction of the Met's new medieval collection.

He called in Charles Collens of the Boston firm Allen, Collens & Willis, whom he had employed to design the Riverside Church in 1930. For that Gothic structure, Collens had traveled to France and Spain, visiting several Gothic churches in order to create a well-informed design. Rockefeller called on him to make a similarly informed plan for the new museum. He and his architect worked with medieval experts, drawing upon the designs of a number of European monasteries and chapels to create a convincing new structure that could sensitively integrate the disparate parts of the collection into one flowing and informative experience.

Throughout the structure new elements were carefully juxtaposed with medieval counterparts. Materials were selected carefully and in many cases handcrafted (when machines would have been more economical) in order to get the most authentic, unified effect. On the exterior, the newly constructed square tower that forms the studio's most recognizable feature was modeled on that of the Benedictine monastery of Saint-Michel-de-Cuxa. Above the exit colonnade an authentic row of lacey refectory windows from the Dominican convent at Sens runs above arches from the cloister of the Benedictine priory at Froville, integrated seamlessly into the rusticated granite facade. Around back, a rounded apse protrudes from the

A view from the covered walkway of the twelfth-century Cuxa Cloister to the central garden and fountain

Detail of Cuxa Cloister column capitals with stylized depictions of vegetation and various beasts

facade. It is a careful replica of the exterior of the apse of San Martín de Fuentadueña, which is contained within these walls. Belgian blocks rescued from demolished New York City streets were recycled to form the fitting, albeit treacherous, drives and sidewalks surrounding the entrances.

Inside, cloisters, chapels, and miscellaneous artifacts are blended almost as seamlessly as they are on the outside. Missing columns are replaced by careful replicas; and a meticulously re-created medieval garden exhibits culinary, artistic, and medicinal plants juxtaposed with the French Bonnefont and Trie Cloisters overlooking the grounds of the park without. Though it is difficult to integrate smaller articles such as chalices and reliquary busts with their surroundings, attempts have been made to do so wherever possible. The rooms containing the famed Unicorn Tapestries (a highly detailed and well-preserved seven-part tapestry series from around 1500 depicting the hunt and capture of the mythical animal) have wooden floors, candelabrum, and pieces of furniture that are reminiscent of the sort of medieval home in which such grand textiles would have been hung.

Due to the nature of the collection, which necessitates the juxtaposition of artifacts from various periods and regions, and the simple fact that these items have been taken out of their original setting, the museum is, of course, not an entirely accurate re-creation. Nonetheless it affords privileged (not to say restricted) access to the art and culture of a period and place very remote from our own, a palpable sense of the very Old World in the midst of the capital of the new.

Rockefeller Center : 1931–1940

West 48th Street to West 51st Street,
between Fifth and Sixth Avenues
The Associated Architects

In 1928, shortly after the Metropolitan Opera Company had run from the eager benefactor William Randolph Hearst, it was drawn to the equally eager—though perhaps more rational—benefactor, John D. Rockefeller, Jr. Like Hearst, Rockefeller wished to construct a cultural center with the opera house as its focal point. Leasing three blocks from Columbia University, which had long since moved to its present campus in Morningside Heights, he set to work immediately with his plans. However, with the onset of the Depression, the opera aborted once again, leaving Rockefeller with an empty plan and a hefty lease at the outset of the worst economic slump the country has ever seen.

An optimistic Rockefeller, in a spirit much like that of John J. Raskob and his iconic Empire State Building, decided to push ahead with his new development based on speculation alone and the belief that if he made the place grand enough, tenants would come. Rockefeller initially hired the architect Harvey Wiley Corbett for the project, but Wallace K. Harrison (a

OPPOSITE: Artist Lee Lawrie's bronze sculpture of Atlas in front of Rockefeller Center's International building, flanked on either side by the twin steeples of St. Patrick's Cathedral across Fifth Avenue

Rockefeller family friend), Raymond Hood, and Reinhard & Hofmeister would all eventually join the planning and design team. Together, the dynamic group came to be known as the Associated Architects, a name that proved rather fitting in the end, when little could be credited solely to any one of them.

Named after its key tenant, the communications megacorporation RCA, the new complex was known as Radio City, and a city it was. The architects, understanding the importance of accessibility and ease of movement, carefully detailed a circulation plan that would not only stitch the complex into the existing urban fabric, but would make navigation within the complex smooth and clear. Their use of mid-block streets represents a tremendous innovation in such planning. These streets, while serving to break down the scale of the existing city grid and impart an inviting sense of intimacy, also allowed pedestrians to move along spacious paths free of the disorienting current of automobile traffic on the avenues. An underground concourse, no doubt adopted from the model of Grand Central, allowed visitors and workers to drop below the congestion of the sidewalks, enjoying shops and restaurants as they made their way to other buildings and streets or to the subway station, which neatly sutured the entire complex to the vast subterranean transportation system.

Understanding the importance of mixed-use, a crucial element in successful urban development, the architects carefully integrated shops, restaurants, theaters, and public spaces into the lower levels. They would not only provide convenience for workers in the office spaces above, but

OPPOSITE: The uninterrupted verticals accentuate the GE Building's height and lighten the mass of the large structure. OVERLEAF: A summertime view of the Rockefeller Plaza and Channel Gardens, with dining umbrellas filling the renowned ice skating rink

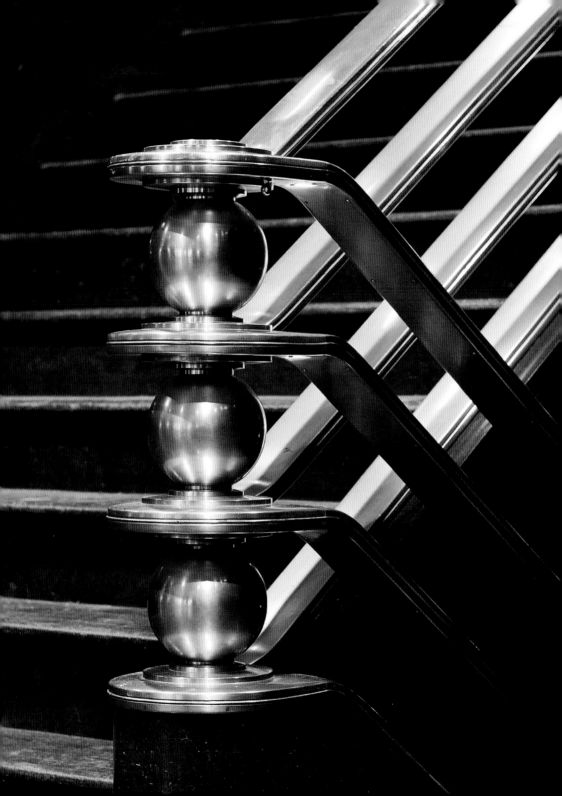

they would serve as a draw for tourists and New Yorkers alike. The shops, which followed the cues of nearby Fifth Avenue establishments in their elegance and richness, wrapped alluringly around corners, quietly drawing people away from the avenue and into the carefully planted and richly ornamented plaza. The Channel Gardens, a lavishly planted row of box gardens flanked by benches, are arranged along the center of the axis running from Fifth Avenue to the plaza and act to further draw strands of the avenue's pedestrian throngs into the center. The theaters are largely arranged along the Avenue of the Americas, closer to the theatrical center of the city around Times Square, where their open frontage on the busy avenue allows the space and visual access necessary for grand advertisement. By incorporating an array of alluring establishments at such carefully selected locations, the architects had sought to ensure all-hours occupation, which would provide revenue when the offices were closed and the sort of energy that would make the center a more attractive place for businesses to settle.

Because of the massive space allotted through the plaza and the mid-block pedestrian streets, the architects could have avoided the use of setbacks on most of the buildings, including the towering central building, now named the General Electric Building. However, due to an interest in the comfort of the office spaces within, the architects opted to maintain the setback tradition. According to the established skyscraper conventions, the number of elevators could decrease as the building rose, since fewer and fewer people would need to go up. This convention freed up considerable

OPPOSITE: The sleek, Art Deco styling of the exterior was carried into the buildings' interiors for everything from murals to lighting fixtures to banisters.

floor space, but it also meant that the desks closer to the elevators would be farther away from the windows and the natural light they allowed. Setbacks, though required in the taller buildings, were not required in the shorter ones. However, since they allowed for the architects to consistently control the distance between the desks and the windows, therefore providing a nearly consistent amount of light to those nearest the elevators on the top floors as at the bottom, setbacks were incorporated into all of the structural forms. These setbacks, at lower levels, would also allow for the provision of landscaped terraces, giving workers a peaceful place to relax during lunch and a lovely view (far better than asphalt and tar) to enjoy throughout the day. This feature, the integration of green public spaces into the office tower, though unprecedented at the time, would soon become one of the defining attributes of tall building construction.

Despite all of these carefully planned details meant to draw businesses and customers into the sparkling new complex, the first few years after completion marked a rather slow start. However, once the Depression had finally begun to lose its hold on the American psyche (as well as the American pocketbook), all of the special amenities would begin to prove worthwhile indeed. Rockefeller's once rather bold and risky venture began to take hold. Today Rockefeller Center stands as one of the city's most renowned destinations.

OPPOSITE: The form of the GE Building seems to rise almost endlessly about the famous Rockefeller Center tree.

United Nations Headquarters : 1953

United Nations Plaza,
First Avenue between East 42nd
and East 48th Streets
Wallace K. Harrison et al.

In 1945, soon after the close of World War II, fifty nations gathered to sign the United Nations Charter, founding an organization that they hoped would indefinitely preserve the new postwar peace. Shortly thereafter the organization's officials set about establishing a permanent headquarters. Though tentative plans were made to build the new headquarters on the former site of the New York World's Fair in Queens, many of the UN's members were more keenly interested in settling in Manhattan, the center of the modern world.

A few years earlier, a real estate developer named William Zeckendorf had purchased a number of slaughterhouses and tanneries along the East River with the intention of building his own speculative city rivaling Rockefeller Center to the west. By the time the UN began searching for a new home, Zeckendorf had abandoned his lofty mission and was eager to sell the land to Rockefeller, who was anxious to make the possibility of a Manhattan UN headquarters a reality. He donated the land to the UN, who readily set to work on the design.

OPPOSITE: The impressive edifice of the United Nations Secretariat Building looms over the later Dag Hammarskjold Library pavilion. OVERLEAF: The forms of the United Nations complex reflect upon the rippled surface of Roche, Dinkeloo and Associates' 1976 United Nations Plaza Hotel.

In early 1947 Wallace K. Harrison was placed in charge of the headquarters design board on the basis of his impressive prior accomplishments, including the design of the UN's temporary headquarters in San Francisco, participation in the realization of the magnificent Radio City (Rockefeller Center), and his wartime experience as head of the Office of American Affairs. He chose a ten-member design team of well-known international architects including Oscar Niemeyer, Sven Markelius, and the now architecturally divine Le Corbusier. Together the members agreed that the complex should be designed in the modern International Style. Replacing the clutter, impracticality, and eclecticism of the patrician Beaux-Arts architecture, it was to be an honest, universal architecture using methods that could be applied to any building with any function in any place, based on the replication of simple geometry, the idea of mass production, and the absence of extraneous ornamentation. Despite its introduction in the U.S. fifteen years prior, the International Style had yet to take off in the States, but its ideology made it ideal for the headquarters of this new international organization whose main goal was to promote an enduring global peace.

The original plan, which closely resembled a 1947 design for the complex by Le Corbusier known as 23a, consisted of three main buildings: the Secretariat, which housed offices and small conference areas for the delegates; the Conference Building, with larger conference areas and dining facilities; and the General Assembly building, which would contain the official hall for the meeting of the General Assembly of all delegates. The Secretariat required the most floor space and therefore the largest structure, and was given a central location. Rising above a clear, open base, the broad east and west facades are formed for the most part by the repetition of its simple heat-absorbent glass windows and transoms, broken only at three intervals by bands of aluminum grids that conceal utilities. The narrow north and south facades are completely clad in a rich, variegated Vermont marble imparting a textured, almost textile appearance, mitigating the otherwise monolithic, windowless planes.

Along the East River, just east of the Secretariat and wrapping around its northern facade, sits the low, solid Conference Building. Organized into simple stacked layers containing three major conference areas and some smaller dining areas, the structure's most significant architectural attribute is the way it connects the Secretariat and the General Assembly, two rather disparate forms.

The General Assembly is a low-lying sculptural building whose sides and roof curve smoothly outward and upward toward its northern facade. Oddly, it is in this windowless northern facade that the architects located the structure's main entrance, rather than in the southern facade, which faces the complex's central plaza. The southern face also contains the only glass in the building, and as such creates an important visual connection between this structure and the plaza, as well as with the buildings around it.

The Dag Hammarskjöld Library, which was added in 1961, faces the southern facade of the General Assembly from across the plaza. Its main facade is primarily glass, and with no transoms to announce the transition between floors, the effect of its main volume is that of one very large, divided light window, very similar to that of the General Assembly. Its other facades are uniformly clad in heavily streaked white stone that alleviates the monotony of these unbroken, windowless expanses with its rich texture. A sloped, pagoda-like attic undermines its otherwise boxy quality.

OVERLEAF: The irregularly waving flags of the world set an interesting contrast to the rigidly gridded facade of the Secretariat Building.

Despite the rather dissimilar character of these elements, their juxta-position yields a series of rather intriguing and well-balanced composi-tions, depending on the viewer's vantage point. From the north, the sculptural lines of the General Assembly hide behind its strictly orthogonal northern facade, and the overall appearance is that of overlaid, differently textured and colored rectangles, enhanced by the smoke stacks rising beyond. From the west, across First Avenue, the compact structures of the General Assembly, Library, and Conference Buildings seem to form a light, desert landscape from which the bulk of the cool green sea of the Secretariat's glass rises. From every angle, the composition is different, yet always simple, balanced, easily comprehensible. The UN brought the International Style to America, and the International Style brought to the UN an architectural statement of its own ideology: unification of disparate, multifaceted parts through honesty, communication, and simplicity of pur-pose, all around a common forum.

Lever House : 1952

390 Park Avenue

Skidmore, Owings & Merrill

The Lever House represents the first attempt in New York to adapt International Style ideals to the urban landscape and the rigors of strict zoning codes. Lever Brothers is a company of British origins that had settled into a headquarters just outside of Boston upon its arrival in the United States in 1890. However, with the company's rapid success in this country (due in major part to its new synthetic detergent Tide), Lever executives succumbed to the irresistible draw of Manhattan. Not wanting to be overlooked in the midst of commercial competitors, they envisioned a sleek new headquarters that would speak for their company—right on the cutting edge of the household products market. They contracted Skidmore, Owings & Merrill, an up-and-coming firm with a tendency toward the modern, whose chief designer, Gordon Bunshaft, in close cooperation with Lever's CEO Charles Luckman, immediately went to work on the design.

One of the most influential modernist prototypes, coming out of 1920s European Modernism, was that of "the tower in the park," a plan

with slim rectilinear towers, elevated on columns to allow for passage below, rising above an expansive green suburban setting. This spacial arrangement was conceived as a foil to and improvement upon the dense urban fabric of places like New York, not as a form to be integrated into its urban setting. Indeed, except in the case of the Secretariat of the UN, which grandly benefited from an uncommonly large site capable of accommodating copious park space, the dense concrete fabric of New York had proven almost completely hostile to the modernist form. Bunshaft, unlike the privileged UN team, was confined to a Manhattan plot of more common dimension, bounded by Park Avenue, Fifty-third, and Fifty-fourth Streets. Thus, rather than designing a tower in the park, Bunshaft designed a park in his tower.

With the broad base raised above street level, pedestrians could move freely below the mass and around the small central garden. Because the company, unlike so many others, had only desired to build as much space as was necessary for its own use (without the provision of additional rentable floor space), Bunshaft had the luxury of using only a small part of the site. He was therefore able to arrange his tower off to one end of his hovering base. This unprecedented under-construction not only exempted the architect from integrating setbacks into his tower design, but left the structure relatively free of obstructions to air and light, maximizing the amount of natural light in the glazed spaces. Plus, with the tower off to one side, the large plane of the base was left open for planting. Giving way at the center for a lightwell that provided light and air to the garden and

OVERLEAF: The cool green Lever tower hovers over its broad base—a pioneer of the "underbuilt" Manhattan site.

spaces below, the arrangement gave the impression from above of bright, luxuriously layered gardens.

The tower itself, true to International Style ideals regarding materials and general design, was clad almost completely in blue-green glass spandrel and window panels held by aluminum and steel supporting members. Though the city's fire codes had required that each transom be backed by a fire retardant brick wall, which interrupted the transparency of the glass planes, the greatest allowable amount of unobstructed glazing provided for considerable natural light by day and the effect of a shimmering crystalline volume by night.

In the end, Bunshaft had not only satisfied his clients with a clean and simple, yet cutting-edge new headquarters, but he had created an unprecedentedly faithful work of modern architecture, with all its simplicity, lightness, and humanity, within the context of the looming city.

Due to an extensive recent restoration overseen by Skidmore, Owings & Merrill that overhauled the structure's distinctive curtain wall (many panels of which had throughout the years been replaced with different colored glass after they had cracked as a result of age-related stresses), the Lever House appears on its fiftieth anniversary as fresh as it did when Bunshaft saw it to completion in 1952.

Seagram Building : 1958

375 Park Avenue
Ludwig Mies van der Rohe
with Philip Johnson

Four years after the completion of the remarkable Lever House—and just one block south—the famed German modernist Ludwig Mies van der Rohe, known for his minimalist forms and simple, yet materially rich and complex architecture, erected his only Manhattan building, providing the city with an uncommon example of finely detailed Modern architecture.

In 1956 Samuel Bronfman, chairman of the board of the Seagram Company, launched plans to build a luxurious new headquarters building in New York, to commemorate the company's impending hundredth anniversary. After some initial sketches by Bronfman's architects had proved unsatisfactory for such a structure, he put his daughter, Phyllis Lambert, in charge of finding the perfect architect. Shortly thereafter, Mies was contracted for the design. Philip Johnson, who organized the Museum of Modern Art's 1932 International Style Exhibition, which had first brought America's attention to Mies's architecture, was soon drawn in by the chief architect to assist with the design.

OVERLEAF: A view across the Seagram Building's plaza. **OVERLEAF #2**: The creamy, polished travertine planes of the lobby dissolve into one another, creating a paradoxically light, nearly immaterial space below the weight of the grand Seagram tower.

Working with a site larger than that of Bunshaft's Lever House but considerably smaller than that of the UN headquarters, Mies adapted the "tower in the park" paradigm to fit his means. An expansive travertine podium along Park Avenue served as the "park" within which his tower was situated, and also provided enough public space to satisfy the city's current zoning regulations. The latter was significant not only because it allowed him to abide for the most part by the Modernist call for simple geometric form, allowing the building to rise, uninterrupted, for thirty-nine stories, but also because it set a precedent for the tower-cum-public plaza form that would proliferate in the decades to come, changing New York's essential fabric forever.

The tower though, however formally ideal it may have been, lacked the provision of sufficient floor space for company use, and a taller tower would not have been possible without integrating setbacks. By symmetrically arranging three low-lying volumes to the tower's rear, Mies was able to incorporate the necessary space without undermining the significance of the tower. A long, opaque spine runs the full height of the tower forging a connection between the tower and the taller secondary volume known as the bustle, which hides directly behind the tower. Because this spine is clad in similar materials with the same rhythms and patterns as the main structure, it is in fact difficult to notice that one ends and the other begins. On either side of the spine and bustle, lower volumes provide all of the necessary additional floor space. Due in part to the successful integration of these separate volumes through stylistic and material continuity, and because the wings rest on lower ground than the raised plaza platform,

OPPOSITE: Ludwig Mies van der Rohe's only New York building, the Seagram Building was the harbinger of the city's most prevalent corporate building idiom—the sleek glass box.

Mies had managed to provide significant additional space while barely disturbing the simple yet elegant geometry of the tower-plaza arrangement. In fact, those looking at the Seagram Building from Park Avenue can scarcely perceive any of the appended volumes beyond the central structure.

Aside from this formal triumph and the structure's significance in the tower-in-plaza trend in New York architecture, the story of the Seagram Building cannot be told without mention of the architect's exceptionally elegant use of materials. Though Seagram's uncommonly large budget provided the architect with a unique opportunity for such treatment, the sensitivity and grace with which Mies employed the materials at his disposal cannot be denied. Heavy slabs of highly textured and subtly colored marble serve to frame and bring warmth to the open expanse of the plaza. The massive columns that hold the tower above its glass lobby, as well as the thin beams that form the structure of the curtain wall, are not of cold steel but coated in rich bronze that complements the bronze tones of the glass and serve generally to soften and warm the entire structure.

As one enters the building, the weight of its dark metallic exterior melts into the creamy white, unembellished travertine planes of the lobby (designed by Johnson). From without, the glass that encloses this space acts as a mirror by day, giving the impression that the plaza continues on into the building, under the weight of the tower above. At night the space glows outward from below the heavy structure, suggesting that the towering structure has somehow overcome the laws of physics, hovering over the plaza on impossibly thin columns. Though such material manipulation and attention to detail had been a constant presence in Mies's designs, the Seagram Building would be the first and last example of his work in New York, arguably his greatest masterpiece.

Solomon R. Guggenheim Museum : 1959

1071 Fifth Avenue

Frank Lloyd Wright

W hen Solomon R. Guggenheim commissioned Frank Lloyd Wright to design a building to house his collection of modern masterworks in 1943, he envisioned a structure that was itself as much a work of art as it was a museum. Though the site was not determined until several months after the design process began, Wright recognized the likelihood that it would be somewhere on the island of Manhattan, where spatial constraints would not allow for the sort of low, sprawling structures that characterized much of his work. Thus, he set to work on a design that would proceed upward, rather than outward. Wright would not be content to stack floors one after another until he achieved some necessary amount of square footage. To him such an arrangement was ill-suited to the structure's basic function. The purpose of a museum or an exhibition space was not simply to provide walls upon which to hang paintings and floors upon which to display sculpture, it was a place to *experience* art, to proceed through the artwork in a continuous fashion, never losing your focus, until

OVERLEAF: An inverted version of the smooth, spiraling design that distinguishes the form of the main gallery was conceived by Frank Lloyd Wright in 1924 in his sketches for an unbuilt tourist attraction in Surgarloaf Mountain, Maryland.

SOLOMON R GUGGENHEIM

the end when you could ruminate upon what you had just beheld. Interruptions caused by extraneous walls, floors, additional accessways, and stairs ran contrary to all of this. Thus, the form of a continuous, spiraling ramp came immediately, fatefully, to the fore; a solution that would not only follow Wright's concept of how art should be experienced but that would create, almost by default, the sort of intriguing, artistic structure that Guggenheim had sought. Sixteen years later, despite the constant resistance of the museum's board after the death of Solomon R. Guggenheim, Wright's staunchest supporter, and six months after the death of the architect himself, a much-revised though all in all Wrightian version of the museum opened its doors in 1959.

Using poured concrete, one of the most manipulable architectural materials, Wright wrapped the outside of the building, merging the low, stacked mass of the monitor building (built mainly for administrative offices) with the towering, cyclonic shell of the main exhibition space, creating one sensuously curving, arrestingly sculptural form. Inside, however, the two forms were almost completely hermetic, their only connections being conceded out of practicality. The intention behind such an arrangement rested with Wright's desire to avoid any potential interruption or distraction along the visitor's path. An elevator carried visitors to the top of the ramp, where, along with the help of gravity, they began their gentle descent, amid the walls and banisters curving in unison as the radius of the ramp spun quietly inward. All the while, the webbed dome above cast magnificent natural light, bathing in warmth and softening the edges of the carefully calculated and controlled space.

OPPOSITE: Natural light floods the interior through Wright's large, central skylight.

Some thirty years later, Wright's beautiful, poetic, and unparalleled masterpiece was in serious need of structural and safety remediation, and the museum was in need of more space. In 1982 Gwathmey Siegel & Associates undertook the demanding and sensitive task of upgrading the work of America's most highly regarded architect. Using lightly colored granite and a tall rectilinear form, the architects sought not to duplicate Wright's style or to extend his design, but rather to complement it with a modest building of their own invention, providing necessary additional floor space with as little intervention into the overall form of the existing structure as possible, and so they did.

Despite this necessary addition and Wright's own extensive revisions to his original design (as a result of museum board members' objections throughout the design and construction process), the Guggenheim Museum stands as the architect's most renowned creation. Today, the power of the central space (despite its alterations)—indeed, the uncanny presence of the entire complex, inside and out—remains every bit as much a Wrightian masterpiece today as it did when it came to life on Wright's drawing board half a century ago.

Lincoln Center : 1962-68

Columbus to Amsterdam Avenues,
from 62nd to 66th Street
Max Ambrovitz, Pietro Belluschi,
Gordon Bunshaft, Walter Gropius,
Wallace K. Harrison, Philip Johnson,
Eero Saarinen

In 1955 the area formerly known as San Juan Hill, just above Columbus
Circle, was slated for urban renewal, a designation that in this, the era of
the powerful and aggressive commissioner Robert Moses, generally meant
large-scale "slum clearance," followed by the construction of new residential, commercial, and cultural structures that would ideally form an instant
neighborhood. That year the city made a tentative arrangement whereby
the Metropolitan Opera Company, which after half a century of foiled plans
was still in search of a new home, would serve as the cultural center of this
latest urban renewal project.

In that same year, the owners of Carnegie Hall announced their decision to demolish their decaying structure in favor of a revenue-producing
office tower (the structure was eventually saved from this fate in the 1960s
due in large part to the efforts of the violinist Isaac Stern), a decision that
left Carnegie's longtime tenant, the New York Philharmonic, homeless. And
so the Philharmonic, in search of a site for its new home (its first official
home), would become a part of the city's new plan.

OVERLEAF: The regular forms of the New York State Theater, the Metropolitan
Opera House, and Avery Fisher Hall, arranged symmetrically around the square,
recall heavily the aesthetic of Italian Renaissance and Classical plazas.

By 1959, when President Eisenhower broke ground for construction, the plan had developed significantly. Lincoln Center for the Performing Arts had been incorporated with John D. Rockefeller, Jr., poised at the helm (and providing significant funding) as president. He transformed the project into the creation of a powerful cultural institution, not just the prospect of two independently acting cultural establishments. The Center's number of cultural constituents had risen, and the large plot between Sixty-second and Sixty-fifth Streets, just off Broadway, had been purchased from the city.

Six architects were chosen to execute the project: Wallace K. Harrison and his partner, Max Ambrovitz, both of whom had been involved with the realization of Rockefeller Center thirty years earlier, and later the United Nations headquarters; Pietro Belluschi, the Italian architect who had cooperated with Walter Gropius on the design of the Met Life Building over Grand Central Terminal; Philip Johnson, the man who brought the International Style to American attention and who had worked with Mies van der Rohe on the Seagram Building; Gordon Bunshaft, known for his canonical Lever House; and Eero Saarinen, who had created the dynamic TWA Terminal at JFK International Airport. Though before this commission they had all largely adhered to the Modern or International Styles, both of which represent antihistorical architecture, each architect succeeded combining elements of both Classical and Modern styles. This unique hybrid style is at the root of Lincoln Center's arresting character.

The entire complex is clad in the distinct Roman travertine that was used in the monuments of Rome's forum, immediately establishing a

Classical quality. Surrounding the central fountain, Abramovitz's Avery Fisher Hall, Johnson's New York State Theater, and Harrison's Metropolitan Opera House, with their stately colonnades, certainly enhance the Classical sense of the complex, and yet the spacious glass volumes within and the abstract forms that replace traditional chandeliers are distinctly Modernist. Around the second plaza, the forms of Belluschi's Juilliard School and Saarinen and Bunshaft's repertory theater and library take on a more straightforwardly Modern appearance, and yet their massing, the way that they enclose the plaza, and their heavy travertine formal elements all harken back to the more overt Classicism of the main plaza. Though the elements of the Classical and the Modern clearly manifest themselves in different manners in each building, the constant interplay between the two styles—and the formal organization around the plazas—gives the complex a striking overall unity. And with the advent of zoning laws giving allowances for additional floor space to developers in the area who incorporated public spaces in the form of colonnades and plazas, the entire vicinity surrounding the complex takes on the distinctive character of the Lincoln Center complex.

OVERLEAF: The Modern tendency toward the creation of volume (away from the creating masses) can be clearly seen in the buildings of Lincoln Center, including Wallace K. Harrison's Metropolitan Opera House, where a simple cubic form becomes the container for a bright, elegant, open volume.

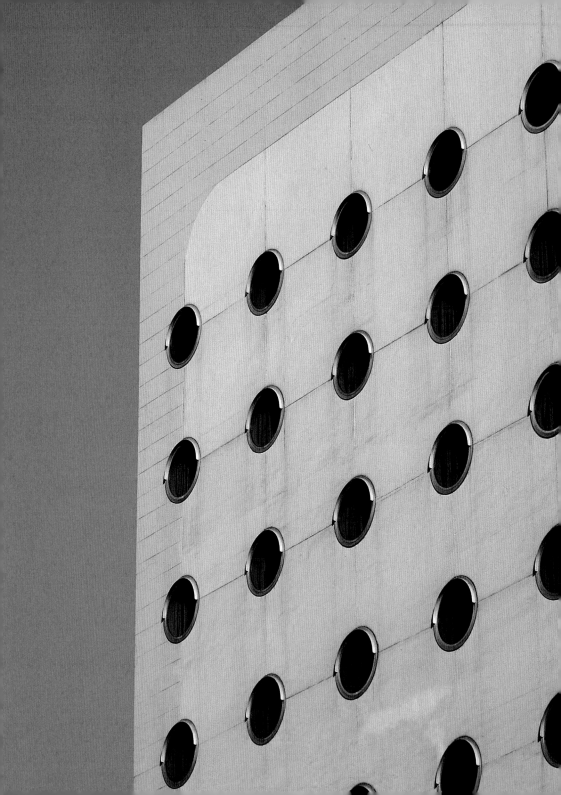

National Maritime Union of America, Joseph Curran Plaza : 1966

100 Ninth Avenue

Albert C. Ledner & Associates

Many of the works in this book are by architects who made their careers by building extensively, if not exclusively, in this city and who perhaps through familiarity and an acquired sensitivity to the city's character have realized some of its most significant structures. However, as can be seen in the singular New York works of such architects as Mies van der Rohe and Frank Lloyd Wright, it does not necessarily take a New York architect to create a significant New York building: In fact, in many cases the fresh insights of the unacquainted outsider form the basis of architectural innovation. When Albert C. Ledner designed the National Maritime Union's Joseph Curran Plaza, he had designed several structures for the Union, one of which was the National Maritime Union Hall on Seventh Avenue between Twelfth and Thirteenth Streets—a structure that, with its reverse setbacks and scalloped crenellations, exemplified Ledner's personal brand of whimsical modern eclecticism. But despite this experience Ledner was still a relative outsider, particularly with regard to building tall struc-

OPPOSITE: The distinctive portholes of Albert C. Ledner's facade are suggestive of its maritime associations.

tures regulated by New York's strict zoning codes. According to these codes the twelve-story dormitory and health facility of the Curran building required setbacks after a certain rise. Ledner, however, avoided the typical, stepped setback configuration by gently tapering the north and south facades into smooth white curves. Framed by ochre tiles and punctured at regular intervals by porthole windows that recall the nautical association of the client, these gently curved planes look less like the facades of a building than they do simple geometric planes in a Cubist painting or sculpture.

Though it may be argued that building such a large-scale sculptural form in the midst of a neighborhood characterized by low-lying, turn-of-the-century brick structures is rather insensitive, it is difficult to deny the significance of Ledner's unique setback solution. Up to this point, the inclusion of public space had been the preferred method for avoiding traditional stepped setbacks, but with this one gesture, Ledner helped to spawn a new line of thinking, whereby the manipulation of form served as the basis for satisfaction of zoning codes.

Trump Tower : 1983

725 Fifth Avenue

Swanke Hayden Connell

Beginning with Jacob Raskob's record-breaking Empire State Building and continuing up the avenue to Rockefeller's impressive Radio City, the city's speculative building legacy, which has yielded some of its most impressive structures, lined the fashionable Fifth Avenue. When Donald Trump secured the Bonwit Teller department store along with its prized site at Fifty-sixth Street and Fifth Avenue in 1979, thus began the creation of a more recent entry into that influential speculative history.

Designed by Der Scutt of Swanke Hayden Connell, Trump's sleek glass tower is cut away at its most visible, southwest corner by vertical setbacks that fall into a cascade of landscaped terraces. This striking detail sets the tower apart from the ubiquitous glass block, creating a 1980s take on promotion through architectural form that was pioneered by the designers of the Tower's venerable speculative ancestors. Inside, a six-story shopping and dining courtyard further recalls idioms of Rockefeller Center and the Empire State Building and their internal concourses. With its impressive

OVERLEAF, LEFT: Trump Tower's cascade of setbacks draws attention from the street. **OVERLEAF, RIGHT:** Warren & Wetmore's 1921 Beaux Arts Heckscher Building (now the Crown Building) contrasts with the black, glass sheen of Trump Tower.

skylight, five-story waterfall, high-society boutiques, and so much bronze-tone mirror and rich orange marble that it is often difficult to find where one surface ends and another begins, the retail courtyard speaks to exactly the sort of business and residential tenants that Trump hoped to draw into the multimillion-dollar suites above. In their expansiveness and opulence, the apartments recall the lineage of such well-known New York apartment buildings as Harde and Short's Alwyn Court and Henry Hardenbergh's Dakota Apartments.

Trump Tower has often been criticized as gaudy and inherently exclusive (despite its nominally public space), and a failure in terms of its commercial space, which is now somewhat desolate in terms of tenants and customers. Yet there is no denying that Trump's creation earned enough overall success to enable him to build several more towers around the city, including the Trump International Hotel at Columbus Circle and the controversial new nine-hundred-fifty-foot Trump World Building, which some have argued to be an affront to the architectural purity of the far East Side, having hitherto been dominated by the UN's Secretariat Building. With its overtly rich and daringly pompous character, Trump Tower has become one of New York's most talked-about buildings.

OPPOSITE: The opulent interior courtyard has been criticized for its inherent exclusivity and for what some deem to be garish décor.

TRUMP TOWER : 172 | 173

ABOVE: The dizzying lattice of the Javits Center's shell from inside
OVERLEAF: The reflective glass, which is transparent from the structure's interior, appears nearly opaque from without, giving the structure the appearance of a tremendous obsidian gem.

Jacob K. Javits
Convention Center : 1986

Eleventh to Twelfth Avenues,
from 34th to 37th Street
I. M. Pei & Partners

By the late 1970s nearly every major American city boasted a colossal, new, state-of-the-art convention center; New York, with its out-moded and outsized Coliseum at Columbus Circle, was not among them. To compete for the considerable revenue created by conventions and exhibitions, the city would have to follow suit. Though a number of sites were considered for the structure, eventually the area between Thirty-fourth and Thirty-seventh Streets and Eleventh and Twelfth Avenues, comprising more than eighteen acres, emerged as the most favorable.

In 1979 James Freed, chief architect of I. M. Pei & Partners, set to work on the design. Taking inspiration from Joseph Paxton's canonical metal-and-glass Crystal Palace of 1851, Freed rejected the unattractive monolithic convention center norm to create a glass-clad space-frame pavilion in which visitors could relax, dine, or enjoy panoramic views of the city when facing the inevitable necessity of waiting in line. By day, the dark glass cladding gives the exterior the appearance of an opaque obsidian gem,

ABOVE: The hermetic concrete volumes of the interior make a limited appearance outside of the Javits Center's distinctive glass shell. OVERLEAF: The concourse glimpsed through the main entrance

reflecting light from its many facets. But as the sun sets, the skin becomes a transparent shell through which one can discern the true logic of the structure: that this complicated glass-and-steel superstructure that gives the building its overall architectural identity is little more than an elaborate pavilion encasing a windowless concrete building within, much like the nondescript, monolithic convention center idiom that Freed sought to avoid. Though this configuration may seem unnecessary or excessive, Freed has really given New York the best of both worlds—one of architectural ingenuity and grace, the other of bottom line, practical construction. For despite the unappealing aesthetics of the standard convention center monolith, it serves its purpose well, providing vast spaces for the exhibition of an architectural blandness that is sure not to distract customers from the business at hand: commerce.

While some have argued that the appearance of a convention center should never have required so much time or complexity, Freed understood otherwise. He recognized that the Javits Center would hold a unique role in forming an image of New York for the many thousands of people that visit for conventions or exhibitions, and with his unique design, he ensured that that image would be positive.

Louis Vuitton, Moët Hennessy (LVMH) Building : 1999

19 East 57th Street

Christian de Portzamparc

As the construction booms of the 1920s, 1950s, 1970s, and 1980s have filled virtually every permissible corner site in Manhattan, it has become nearly impossible, if not economically restrictive, for institutions to build on such privileged sites. The result has been an increase in the development of more limited, mid-block sites, which offer proximity to city centers without the cost of a corner lot. Such is the case with the 1999 headquarters building for the French-based Louis Vuitton, Moët Hennessy luxury goods megagroup, which rises from a narrow site along Fifty-seventh Street, just east of the glamorous Fifth Avenue shopping district. However, the twenty-three-story structure, designed by Pritzker Prize–winning French architect Christian de Portzamparc, gracefully transcends any of the limitations wrought by the size and location of the site, standing as one of the most intriguing and visible structures in the area, and perhaps the entire city.

In much the same way as one of the client's designers would have fashioned a garment, de Portzamparc pushed, pulled, cut, and joined a glass cur-

OPPOSITE: The delicately textured glass curtain wall of the LVMH Tower wraps the interior in an elegant, luminous cloak.

tain wall to create a structure to satisfy New York's powerful setback building codes, while avoiding the traditional methods of regularly stacked masses or gentle slopes. The sculptural product of this tailoring was carefully detailed by the juxtaposition of clear, low-iron glass panels with more traditional blue-green glass panels that are variously left clear, sandblasted with simple geometric forms, or treated with baked-on ceramic patterns, providing a unique pattern of textures and colors. Each floor gently tapers as it approaches the façade, reducing its manifestation there and thus maximizing the continuity of the glass cloak.

From afar the cool green volume rises provocatively above the heavy, masonry-clad masses surrounding it, and from more oblique angles its brilliant facets break the bland plane of the street facades that line up in either direction, thoroughly dominating the northern side of the street. Through careful attention to detail and the creative manipulation of zoning codes, de Portzamparc not only created a stylish headquarters befitting his client, but a new standard for New York architecture, showing that mid-block limitations may inevitably yield some of the city's finest and most creative architecture yet.

Bibliography

Atkinson, Fello. "Six Recent Buildings in the USA." *Architects' Yearbook* 5 (1953): 133–41, 142–45, 133–69.

Belle , John, and Maxinne R. Leighton. *Grand Central: Gateway to a Million Lives.* New York: W. W. Norton & Company, 2000.

Berktold, Ruth. "Christian de Portzamparc: LVMH Tower Building, New York." *Domus*, February 2000, 16–21.

Carnegie Corporation of New York website, www.carnegie.org.

Christen, Barbara, and Steven Flanders, eds. *Cass Gilbert, Life and Work: Architect of the Public Domain.* New York: W. W. Norton & Company, 2001.

Collins, Brad, ed. *Gwathmey Siegel: Buildings and Projects 1965-2000.* New York: Universe Publishing, 2000.

Constantino, Maria. *The Life and Works of Frank Lloyd Wright.* London: PRC Publishing, Ltd., 1998.

Cornachio, Donna. "Chelsea Controversy." *Metropolis*, November 1987, 24.

DeLony, Eric. *Landmark American Bridges.* New York: American Society of Civil Engineers, 1993.

Dierickx, Mary B., research consultant. *The Bayard (Condict) Building.* New York: Office of Joseph Pell Lombardi, architect (AA 735 N4 L833).

Dietsch, Deborah K. "Space Frame Odyssey: Jacob K. Javits Convention Center, New York City." *Architectural Record*, September 1986, 106–16.

Dolkart, Andrew. *Guide to New York City Landmarks*. Washington, D.C.: The Preservation Press, 1992.

Fitch, James Marston. "Renovation of Alwyn Court, New York City: Restoring the Facades and Improving Public Spaces." *Technology & Conservation*, summer 1980, 24–27.

"George Washington Bridge." *Architectural Record*, www.archrecord.construction.com/Lighting/may01/gwbridge.asp.

A Guide to New Orleans Architecture. New Orleans: American Institute of Architects, New Orleans Chapter, 1974.

Hart, Sara. "LVMH: Making Things Perfectly Clear," *Architecture*, March 2000.

"Hearst Magazine Building." *Wired New York*, www.wirednewyork.com/real_estate/hearst_magazine_building/default.htm.

"A Hero Finds Rest." *The New York Times*, 24 July 1885.

Jackson, Kenneth T., ed. *The Encyclopedia of New York City*. New Haven, Conn.: Yale University Press, 1995.

Krinsky, Carol Herselle. *Rockefeller Center*. Oxford: Oxford University Press, 1978.

Lamb, Brian. *Who's Buried in Grant's Tomb? A Tour of Presidential Gravesites*. Washington, D.C.: National Cable Satellite Corporation, 2000.

Landau, Sarah Bedford, and Carl W. Condit. *The Rise of the New York Skyscraper, 1865–1913.* New Haven: Yale University Press, 1996.

Landmarks Preservation Commission of the City of New York, LP-0674 (Andrew Carnegie Mansion, 2/19/1974); no. 4.

Landmarks Preservation Commission of the City of New York, LP-0828 (Queensboro Bridge, 4/16/1974); no. 2.

Landmarks Preservation Commission of the City of New York, LP-0835 (The Cloisters, 3/19/1974); no. 4.

Landmarks Preservation Commission of the City of New York, LP-0992 (Chrysler Building, 9/12/1978); designation list 118.

Landmarks Preservation Commission of the City of New York, LP-0996 (Chrysler Building Lobby, 9/12/1978); designation list 118.

Landmarks Preservation Commission of the City of New York, LP-1050 (McGraw-Hill Building, 9/11/1979); designation list 127.

Landmarks Preservation Commission of the City of New York, LP-1099 (Grand Central Terminal Interior, 9/23/1980); designation list 137.

Landmarks Preservation Commission of the City of New York, LP-1226 (Puck Building, 4/12/1983); designation list 164.

Landmarks Preservation Commission of the City of New York, LP-1277 (Lever House, 11/9/1982); designation list 161.

Landmarks Preservation Commission of the City of New York, LP-1625 (Hearst Magazine Building, 2/16/1988); designation list 200.

Landmarks Preservation Commission of the City of New York, LP-1664 (Seagram Building, 10/3/1989), designation list 221.

Landmarks Preservation Commission of the City of New York, LP-1666 (Four Seasons Restaurant, 10/3/1989); designation list 221.

Loeffler, Jane C. Introduction to *The United Nations,* by Ezra Stoller, ed. New York: Princeton Architectural Press, 1999.

Mendelsohn, Joyce. *Touring the Flatiron: Walks in Four Historic Neighborhoods.* New York Landmarks Conservancy, 1998.

Muschamp, Herbert. "A Crystal Beacon Atop a 20's Curiosity." *New York Times*, 30 October 2001.

Nevins, Deborah, ed. *Grand Central Terminal: City within the City.* The Municipal Art Society of New York, 1982.

Opening Week of Lincoln Center for the Performing Arts: Philharmonic Hall, program, 23–30 September 1962 (AA735 N4 ZL633).

Pfeiffer, Bruce Brooks. *Frank Lloyd Wright: Master Builder.* New York: Universe Publishing, 1997.

Plunz, Richard. *A History of Housing in New York City: Dwelling Type and Social Change in the American Metropolis.* New York: Columbia University Press, 1990.

Preston, Douglas. "Chianti Postcard: A Verrazano Tribute." *New Yorker*, 8 July 2002, 25–26.

Rastorfer, Darl. *Six Bridges: The Legacy of Othmar H. Ammann*. New Haven, Conn.: Yale University Press, 2000.

Reed, Henry Hope. *Beaux-Arts Architecture in New York City: A Photographic Guide*. Mineola, N.Y.: Dover Publications, 1988.

Reed, Henry Hope. *Rockefeller New York: A Tour*. New York: Greensward Foundation, Inc., 1988.

Rorimer, James J. *Medieval Monuments at the Cloisters: As They Were and As They Are*. Rev. ed. by Katherine Serrell Rorimer. New York: The Metropolitan Museum of Art, 1972.

Rouda, Mitchell B. "Dazzling, Problem Plagued 'Crystal Palace': Manhattan's Javits Center." *Architecture: The AIA Journal*, March 1987, 92–101.

Schulze, Franz. Introduction to *The Seagram Building* by Ezra Stoller, ed. New York: Princeton Architectural Press, 1999.

Stern, Robert A. M. *New York 1880: Architecture and Urbanism in the Gilded Age*. New York: The Monacelli Press, 1999.

Stern, Robert A. M. *New York 1900: Metropolitan Architecture and Urbanism 1890–1915*. New York: Rizzoli International Publications, 1983.

Stern, Robert A. M. *New York 1930: Architecture and Urbanism Between the Two World Wars.* New York: Rizzoli International Publications, 1987.

Tauranac, John. *Elegant New York: The Builders and the Buildings 1885–1915.* New York: Abbeville Press, 1985.

Viller, Martin. "High Ruse, Part I." *Art in America*, September 1984, 150–65.

White, Norval, and Elliot Willensky. *AIA Guide to New York City.* New York: Crown Publishers, 2000.

Willis, Carol, ed. *Building the Empire State.* New York: W. W. Norton & Company, 1998.

Willis, Carol. *Form Follows Finance: Skyscrapers and Skylines in New York and Chicago.* New York: Princeton Architectural Press, 1995.

Young, Edgar B. *Lincoln Center: The Building of an Institution.* New York: New York University Press, 1980.